THE YALE SHAKESPEARE

EDITED BY

WILBUR L. CROSS   TUCKER BROOKE

WILLARD HIGLEY DURHAM

PUBLISHED UNDER THE DIRECTION
OF THE
DEPARTMENT OF ENGLISH, YALE UNIVERSITY,
ON THE FUND
GIVEN TO THE YALE UNIVERSITY PRESS IN 1917
BY THE MEMBERS OF THE
KINGSLEY TRUST ASSOCIATION
TO COMMEMORATE THE SEVENTY-FIFTH ANNIVERSARY
OF THE FOUNDING OF THE SOCIETY

THE LIFE OF TIMON OF ATHENS

EDITED BY

STANLEY T. WILLIAMS

LVX ET VERITAS

NEW HAVEN · YALE UNIVERSITY PRESS
LONDON · HUMPHREY MILFORD
OXFORD UNIVERSITY PRESS · MCMXIX

TABLE OF CONTENTS

The facsimile opposite represents the list of Dramatis Personæ as given in the original edition (the Folio of 1623). The list there appears on an otherwise blank page following the close of the play. The photograph has been made from the Elizabethan Club copy of the Folio.

THE
ACTORS
NAMES.

TYMON of Athens.
Lucius, And
Lucullus, two Flattering Lords.
Appemantus, a Churlish Philosopher.
Sempronius another flattering Lord.
Alcibiades, an Athenian Captaine.
Poet.
Painter.
Jeweller.
Merchant.
Certaine Senatours.
Certaine Maskers.
Certaine Theeues.

Flaminius, one of Tymons Seruants.
Seruilius, another.
Caphis.
Varro.
Philo.
Titus.
Lucius.
Hortensis
} Seuerall Seruants to Vsurers.

Ventigius. one of Tymons false Friends.
Cupid.
Sempronius.
With diuers other Seruants,
And Attendants.

[DRAMATIS PERSONÆ.]

TIMON *of Athens*

LUCIUS,
LUCULLUS, } *flattering Lords*
SEMPRONIUS,

VENTIDIUS, *one of Timon's false Friends*
APEMANTUS, *a churlish Philosopher*
ALCIBIADES, *an Athenian Captain*
Poet, Painter, Jeweller, Merchant [and Mercer]
Certain Senators
Certain Masquers [*Ladies dressed as Amazons*]
Certain Thieves
[FLAVIUS, *Steward to Timon*]

FLAMINIUS,
[LUCILIUS,] } *Servants to Timon*
SERVILIUS,

CAPHIS,
PHILOTUS,
TITUS, } *Several Servants to Usurers* [*and to*
LUCIUS, *the Lords*]
HORTENSIUS,

[PHRYNIA,
TIMANDRA, } *Mistresses to Alcibiades*]

CUPID

With divers other Servants and Attendants
[Servants of Ventidius, and of Varro and Isidore
(two of Timon's Creditors)
Three Strangers
An Old Athenian
A Page
A Fool]

[SCENE: *Athens, and the neighbouring Woods.*]

Dramatis Personæ; *cf. n.*

The Life of Timon of Athens

ACT FIRST

Scene One

[Athens.   A Hall in Timon's House]

*Enter Poet, Painter, Jeweller, Merchant, and Mercer,
at several doors.*

Poet. Good day, sir.
Pain.   I am glad you're well.
Poet. I have not seen you long: how goes the
world?
Pain. It wears, sir, as it grows.
Poet.   Ay, that's well known:
But what particular rarity? what strange,   4
Which manifold record not matches? See,
Magic of bounty! all these spirits thy power
Hath conjur'd to attend. I know the merchant.
Pain. I know them both; th' other's a jeweller. 8
Merch. O, 'tis a worthy lord!
Jew.   Nay, that's most fix'd.
Merch. A most incomparable man, breath'd, as it
were,
To an untirable and continuate goodness:
He passes.
Jew.   I have a jewel here—   12
Merch. O, pray, let's see 't: for the Lord Timon,
sir?

Scene One, S. d. and Mercer; *cf. n.*   2 long: *for a long time*
3 grows: *grows older; cf. n.*
4, 5 what strange, etc.: *what unusual event*   9 fix'd: *certain*
10 breath'd: *inured*   11 continuate: *lasting*   12 passes: *surpasses*

Jew. If he will touch the estimate: but, for that—

Poet. 'When we for recompense have prais'd the vile,

It stains the glory in that happy verse   16

Which aptly sings the good.'

    Merch. [*Looking at the jewel.*] 'Tis a good form.

    Jew. And rich: here is a water, look ye.

    Pain. You are rapt, sir, in some work, some dedication

To the great lord.

    Poet.   A thing slipp'd idly from me.   20

Our poesy is as a gum, which oozes

From whence 'tis nourish'd: the fire i' the flint

Shows not till it be struck; our gentle flame

Provokes itself, and, like the current, flies   24

Each bound it chafes. What have you there?

    Pain. A picture, sir. When comes your book forth?

    Poet. Upon the heels of my presentment, sir.

Let's see your piece.   28

    Pain. 'Tis a good piece.

    Poet. So 'tis: this comes off well and excellent.

    Pain. Indifferent.

    Poet.   Admirable: how this grace

Speaks his own standing! what a mental power   32

This eye shoots forth! how big imagination

Moves in this lip! to the dumbness of the gesture

One might interpret.

    Pain. It is a pretty mocking of the life.   36

Here is a touch; is 't good?

    Poet.   I'll say of it,

14 touch the estimate: *pay the price at which it is valued*
15 'When we for recompense,' etc.; *cf. n.*   18 water: *lustre*
19 rapt: *transported*   23-25 our gentle flame . . . chafes; *cf. n.*
27 presentment: *dedication; cf. n.*   30 comes off: *turns out*
31 Indifferent: *reasonably well*   32 standing: *position* (?); *cf. n.*
34 to the dumbness, etc.; *cf. n.*

It tutors nature: artificial strife
Lives in these touches, livelier than life.

   Enter certain Senators [who pass over the stage].

   Pain. How this lord is follow'd!   40
   Poet. The senators of Athens: happy man!
   Pain. Look, moe!
   Poet. You see this confluence, this great flood of
     visitors.
I have, in this rough work, shap'd out a man,   44
Whom this beneath world doth embrace and hug
With amplest entertainment: my free drift
Halts not particularly, but moves itself
In a wide sea of wax: no levell'd malice   48
Infects one comma in the course I hold;
But flies an eagle flight, bold and forth on,
Leaving no tract behind.

   Pain. How shall I understand you?
   Poet.   I will unbolt to you.   52
You see how all conditions, how all minds,
As well of glib and slippery creatures as
Of grave and austere quality, tender down
Their services to Lord Timon: his large fortune,   56
Upon his good and gracious nature hanging,
Subdues and properties to his love and tendance
All sorts of hearts; yea, from the glass-fac'd flatterer
To Apemantus, that few things loves better   60
Than to abhor himself: even he drops down
The knee before him, and returns in peace
Most rich in Timon's nod.

   Pain.   I saw them speak together.

---

38 artificial strife: *vying of art with nature*   42 moe: *more*
44 shap'd out: *imagined*   45 beneath world: *world below*
46 drift: *aim*   47 particularly: *at any individual person*
48 wide sea of wax; *cf. n.*   levell'd: *designed* (?); *cf. n.*
50 forth on: *forward*   51 tract: *track*   52 unbolt: *disclose*
58 properties: *appropriates*   tendance: *service*
59 glass-fac'd: *reflecting, like a mirror, the looks of another*

Poet. Sir, I have upon a high and pleasant hill   64
Feign'd Fortune to be thron'd: the base o' the mount
Is rank'd with all deserts, all kind of natures,
That labour on the bosom of this sphere
To propagate their states: amongst them all,   68
Whose eyes are on this sovereign lady fix'd,
One do I personate of Lord Timon's frame,
Whom Fortune with her ivory hand wafts to her;
Whose present grace to present slaves and servants   72
Translates his rivals.
　　Pain.   'Tis conceiv'd to scope.
This throne, this Fortune, and this hill, methinks,
With one man beckon'd from the rest below,
Bowing his head against the steepy mount   76
To climb his happiness, would be well express'd
In our condition.
　　Poet.   Nay, sir, but hear me on.
All those which were his fellows but of late,
Some better than his value, on the moment   80
Follow his strides, his lobbies fill with tendance,
Rain sacrificial whisperings in his ear,
Make sacred even his stirrup, and through him
Drink the free air.
　　Pain.   Ay, marry, what of these?   84
　　Poet. When Fortune in her shift and change of
　　　　mood
Spurns down her late belov'd, all his dependants
Which labour'd after him to the mountain's top
Even on their knees and hands, let him slip down,   88
Not one accompanying his declining foot.

66 Is rank'd with all deserts: *has men of all kinds standing in rows*
68 states: *fortunes*   70 personate: *represent*
71 wafts: *beckons*   72 present slaves: *immediate slaves*
73 Translates: *transforms*   to scope: *to the purpose*
76 steepy: *difficult to ascend*   77, 78 would . . . condition; *cf. n.*
82 sacrificial: *having the character of sacrifice offered to a god*
84 marry: *by Mary, an oath*

Pain. 'Tis common:
A thousand moral paintings I can show,
That shall demonstrate these quick blows of For-
        tune's   92
More pregnantly than words. Yet you do well
To show Lord Timon that mean eyes have seen
The foot above the head.
*Trumpets sound. Enter Lord Timon, addressing
        himself courteously to every suitor. [A Messen-
        ger from Ventidius talking with him; Lucilius
        and other servants following.]*

Tim.   Imprison'd is he, say you?

Mess. Ay, my good lord: five talents is his debt;   96
Iis means most short, his creditors most strait:
Your honourable letter he desires
To those have shut him up; which failing,
Periods his comfort.

Tim.   Noble Ventidius! Well: 100
I am not of that feather to shake off
My friend when he must need me. I do know him
A gentleman that well deserves a help:
Which he shall have: I'll pay the debt and free
        him.   104

Mess. Your lordship ever binds him.

Tim. Commend me to him: I will send his ransom;
And, being enfranchis'd, bid him come to me.
'Tis not enough to help the feeble up,   108
But to support him after. Fare you well.

Mess. All happiness to your honour!   *Exit.*

Enter an old Athenian.

Old Ath. Lord Timon, hear me speak.

91 moral: *allegorical*   93 pregnantly: *clearly*
94 mean eyes: *eyes of inferiors*   96 five talents; *cf. n.*
97 strait: *exacting*   100 Periods: *brings to an end*

Tim.   Freely, good father.

Old Ath. Thou hast a servant nam'd Lucilius.   112

Tim. I have so: what of him?

Old Ath. Most noble Timon, call the man before
    thee.

Tim. Attends he here, or no? Lucilius!

Luc. Here, at your lordship's service.   116

Old Ath. This fellow here, Lord Timon, this thy
    creature,
By night frequents my house. I am a man
That from my first have been inclin'd to thrift,
And my estate deserves an heir more rais'd   120
Than one which holds a trencher.

Tim.   Well, what further?

Old Ath. One only daughter have I, no kin else,
On whom I may confer what I have got:
The maid is fair, o' the youngest for a bride,   124
And I have bred her at my dearest cost
In qualities of the best. This man of thine
Attempts her love: I prithee, noble lord,
Join with me to forbid him her resort;   128
Myself have spoke in vain.

Tim.   The man is honest.

Old Ath. Therefore he will be, Timon:
His honesty rewards him in itself;
It must not bear my daughter.

Tim.   Does she love him?   132

Old Ath. She is young and apt:
Our own precedent passions do instruct us
What levity's in youth.

120 more rais'd: *of higher station*
121 holds a trencher: *serves at table*   125 dearest: *utmost*
128 her resort: *visiting her by way of courtship*
129-132 The man is honest . . . daughter; *cf. n.*
132 bear: *carry as a consequence*   133 apt: *pliable*
134 precedent: *early*

Tim. [*To Lucilius.*] Love you the maid?

Luc. Ay, my good lord; and she accepts of it.   136

Old Ath. If in her marriage my consent be missing,
I call the gods to witness, I will choose
Mine heir from forth the beggars of the world,
And dispossess her all.

Tim.   How shall she be endow'd,   140
If she be mated with an equal husband?

Old Ath. Three talents on the present; in future,
   all.

Tim. This gentleman of mine hath serv'd me long:
To build his fortune I will strain a little,   144
For 'tis a bond in men. Give him thy daughter:
What you bestow, in him I'll counterpoise,
And make him weigh with her.

Old Ath.   Most noble lord,
Pawn me to this your honour, she is his.   148

Tim. My hand to thee; mine honour on my promise.

Luc. Humbly I thank your lordship: never may
That state or fortune fall into my keeping,
Which is not ow'd to you!   152

                Exit [*with old Athenian*].

Poet. Vouchsafe my labour, and long live your
   lordship!

Tim. I thank you; you shall hear from me anon:
Go not away. What have you there, my friend?

Pain. A piece of painting, which I do beseech   156
Your lordship to accept.

Tim.   Painting is welcome.
The painting is almost the natural man;
For since dishonour traffics with man's nature,
He is but outside: these pencil'd figures are   160

---

140 all: *altogether*
145 bond in men: *obligation of affection among men*
147 weigh: *equivalent in wealth*   148 Pawn: *if you pledge*

Even such as they give out. I like your work,
And you shall find I like it: wait attendance
Till you hear further from me.

 Pain.   The gods preserve ye!

 Tim. Well fare you, gentleman: give me your
  hand;   164

We must needs dine together. Sir, your jewel
Hath suffer'd under praise.

 Jew.   What, my lord! dispraise?

 Tim. A mere satiety of commendations.

If I should pay you for 't as 'tis extoll'd, 168
It would unclew me quite.

 Jew.   My lord, 'tis rated

As those which sell would give: but you well know,
Things of like value, differing in the owners,
Are prized by their masters. Believe 't, dear lord, 172
You mend the jewel by the wearing it.

 Tim. Well mock'd.

Enter Apemantus.

 Merch. No, my good lord; he speaks the common
  tongue,

Which all men speak with him   176

 Tim. Look, who comes here: will you be chid?

 Jew. We'll bear, with your lordship.

 Merch.   He'll spare none.

 Tim. Good morrow to thee, gentle Apemantus!

 Apem. Till I be gentle, stay thou for thy good
  morrow;   180

When thou art Timon's dog, and these knaves honest.

 Tim. Why dost thou call them knaves? thou know'st
  them not.

161 give out: *profess to be*   162 wait attendance: *remain near*
166 Hath . . . dispraise; *cf. n.*   169 unclew: *ruin*
170 As . . . give; *cf. n.*   172 by: *according to*
181 When . . . honest; *cf. n.*

Apem. Are they not Athenians?

Tim. Yes.   184

Apem. Then I repent not.

Jew. You know me, Apemantus?

Apem. Thou know'st I do; I call'd thee by
thy name.   188

Tim. Thou art proud, Apemantus?

Apem. Of nothing so much as that I am not
like Timon.

Tim. Whither art going?   192

Apem. To knock out an honest Athenian's
brains.

Tim. That's a deed thou'lt die for.

Apem. Right, if doing nothing be death by
the law.   197

Tim. How likest thou this picture, Apemantus?

Apem. The best, for the innocence.   200

Tim. Wrought he not well that painted it?

Apem. He wrought better that made the
painter; and yet he's but a filthy piece of work.

Pain. You're a dog.   204

Apem. Thy mother's of my generation:
what's she, if I be a dog?

Tim. Wilt dine with me, Apemantus?

Apem. No; I eat not lords.   208

Tim. An thou shouldst, thou'dst anger ladies.

Apem. O, they eat lords; so they come by
great bellies.

Tim. That's a lascivious apprehension.   212

Apem. So thou apprehendest it: take it for
thy labour.

200 innocence: *stupidity*   209 An: *if*
212 apprehension: *interpretation*

Tim. How dost thou like this jewel, Apemantus?   216

Apem. Not so well as plain-dealing, which
will not cost a man a doit.

Tim. What dost thou think 'tis worth?

Apem. Not worth my thinking. How now,
poet!   221

Poet. How now, philosopher!

Apem. Thou liest.

Poet. Art not one?   224

Apem. Yes.

Poet. Then I lie not.

Apem. Art not a poet?

Poet. Yes.   228

Apem. Then thou liest: look in thy last work,
where thou hast feigned him a worthy fellow.

Poet. That's not feigned; he is so.   231

Apem. Yes, he is worthy of thee, and to pay
thee for thy labour: he that loves to be flattered
is worthy o' the flatterer. Heavens, that I were
a lord!   235

Tim. What wouldst do then, Apemantus?

Apem. Even as Apemantus does now; hate
a lord with my heart.   238

Tim. What, thyself?

Apem. Ay.

Tim. Wherefore?   241

Apem. That I had no angry wit to be a lord.
Art not thou a merchant?

Merch. Ay, Apemantus.   244

Apem. Traffic confound thee, if the gods will
not!

217 plain-dealing; *cf. n.*
218 doit: *a former Dutch coin, equivalent to half a farthing, a trifle*
242 That . . . lord; *cf. n.*

    Merch. If traffic do it, the gods do it.
    Apem. Traffic's thy god; and thy god con-
found thee!   249

      Trumpet sounds. Enter a Messenger.

    Tim. What trumpet's that?
    Mes. 'Tis Alcibiades, and some twenty horse,
All of companionship.   252
    Tim. Pray, entertain them; give them guide to us.
                [Exeunt some Attendants.]
You must needs dine with me: go not you hence
Till I have thank'd you: when dinner's done,
Show me this piece. I am joyful of your sights. 256

    Enter Alcibiades with the rest [of his Company].

Most welcome, sir!
    Apem.   So, so, there!
Aches contract and starve your supple joints!
That there should be small love 'mongst these sweet
    knaves,
And all this courtesy! The strain of man's bred
    out   260
Into baboon and monkey.
    Alcib. Sir, you have sav'd my longing, and I feed
Most hungerly on your sight.
    Tim.   Right welcome, sir!
Ere we depart, we'll share a bounteous time   264
In different pleasures. Pray you, let us in.
              Exeunt [all except Apemantus].

        Enter two Lords.

    First Lord. What time o' day is 't, Apemantus?

252 All of companionship: *all belonging to one party*
258 Aches; *cf. n.*   starve: *paralyze*
260 strain: *stock*   bred out: *degenerated*
263 hungerly: *hungrily*   264 depart: *take leave of one another*

Apem. Time to be honest.

First Lord. That time serves still.   268

Apem. The most accursed thou, that still omitt'st
it.

Sec. Lord. Thou art going to Lord Timon's
feast?

Apem. Ay, to see meat fill knaves and wine heat
fools.   272

Sec. Lord. Fare thee well, fare thee well.

Apem. Thou art a fool to bid me farewell twice.

Sec. Lord. Why, Apemantus?

Apem. Shouldst have kept one to thyself, for
I mean to give thee none.   277

First Lord. Hang thyself!

Apem. No, I will do nothing at thy bidding:
make thy requests to thy friend.   280

Sec. Lord. Away, unpeaceable dog, or I'll
spurn thee hence!

Apem. I will fly, like a dog, the heels o' the
ass.   [*Exit.*]

First Lord. He's opposite to humanity. Come,
shall we in,   285
And taste Lord Timon's bounty? he outgoes
The very heart of kindness.

Sec. Lord. He pours it out; Plutus, the god of
gold,   288
Is but his steward: no meed, but he repays
Sevenfold above itself; no gift to him,
But breeds the giver a return exceeding
All use of quittance.

First Lord.   The noblest mind he carries   292
That ever govern'd man.

268 serves: *affords an opportunity*   281 unpeaceable: *quarrelsome*
285 opposite: *hostile*   286 outgoes: *exceeds*   288 Plutus; *cf. n.*
289 meed: *gift*   292 use of quittance: *customary requital*

Sec. Lord. Long may he live in fortunes!
Shall we in?

First Lord. I'll keep you company.   296

Exeunt.

Scene Two

[*The Same. A Banqueting-room in Timon's House.*]

*Hautboys playing loud music. A great banquet
served in: and then, Enter Lord Timon, the
States, the Athenian Lords, Ventidius which
Timon redeemed from prison. [Enter Alcibiades. Flavius and others attending.] Then
comes, dropping after all, Apemantus, discontentedly, like himself.*

Ven. Most honour'd Timon,
hath pleas'd the gods to remember my father's age,
And call him to long peace.
He is gone happy, and has left me rich: 4
Then, as in grateful virtue I am bound
To your free heart, I do return those talents,
Doubled with thanks and service, from whose help
I deriv'd liberty.

Tim.   O, by no means,   8
Honest Ventidius; you mistake my love:
I gave it freely ever; and there's none
Can truly say he gives, if he receives:
If our betters play at that game, we must not dare   12
To imitate them; faults that are rich are fair.

Ven. A noble spirit!

[*They all stand ceremoniously looking on Timon.*]

Scene Two, S. d. States: *princes*   which: *whom*   dropping after
     all: *lingering*

Tim. Nay, my lords, ceremony was but devis'd at
   first
To set a gloss on faint deeds, hollow welcomes,   16
Recanting goodness, sorry ere 'tis shown;
But where there is true friendship, there needs none.
Pray, sit; more welcome are ye to my fortunes
Than my fortunes to me.   [*They sit.*]
   First Lord. My lord, we always have confess'd
      it.   21
   Apem. Ho, ho, confess'd it! hang'd it, have you
      not?
   Tim. O, Apemantus, you are welcome.
   Apem.   No;
You shall not make me welcome: 24
I come to have thee thrust me out of doors.
   Tim. Fie, thou'rt a churl; ye've got a humour there
Does not become a man; 'tis much to blame.
They say, my lords, 'Ira furor brevis est';   28
But yond man is ever angry.
Go, let him have a table by himself;
For he does neither affect company,
Nor is he fit for 't, indeed.   32
   Apem. Let me stay at thine apperil, Timon:
I come to observe; I give thee warning on 't.
   Tim. I take no heed of thee; thou'rt an
Athenian, therefore, welcome: I myself would
have no power; prithee, let my meat make thee
silent.   38
   Apem. I scorn thy meat; 'twould choke me, for I
      should
Ne'er flatter thee. O you gods, what a number   40
Of men eat Timon, and he sees 'em not!

21, 22 confess'd . . . not; *cf. n.*   26 humour: *disposition*
28-44; *cf. n.*   28 'Ira furor brevis est'; *cf. n.*   31 affect: *like*
33 apperil: *risk*   37 power: *i.e., to make you silent*

It grieves me to see so many dip their meat
In one man's blood; and all the madness is,
He cheers them up too.   44
I wonder men dare trust themselves with men:
Methinks they should invite them without knives;
Good for their meat, and safer for their lives.
There's much example for 't; the fellow that   48
Sits next him now, parts bread with him, and pledges
The breath of him in a divided draught,
Is the readiest man to kill him: 't has been prov'd.
If I were a huge man, I should fear to drink at
    meals,   52
Lest they should spy my wind-pipe's dangerous notes:
Great men should drink with harness on their throats.
   Tim. My lord, in heart; and let the health go
    round.
   Sec. Lord. Let it flow this way, my good lord.   56
    Apem. Flow this way! A brave fellow! he
keeps his tides well. Those healths will make
thee and thy state look ill, Timon.
Here's that which is too weak to be a sinner,   60
Honest water, which ne'er left man i' the mire:
This and my food are equals; there's no odds:
Feasts are too proud to give thanks to the gods.

Apemantus's Grace.

  ' Immortal gods, I crave no pelf;   64
    I pray for no man but myself:
    Grant I may never prove so fond,
    To trust man on his oath or bond,
    Or a harlot for her weeping,   68
    Or a dog that seems a-sleeping,

---

46 Methinks . . . knives; *cf. n.*   47 Good: *that would be good*
53 dangerous notes: *signs of vulnerability*   54 harness: *armor*
55 in heart: *cheer up*   66 fond: *foolish*

Or a keeper with my freedom;
Or my friends, if I should need 'em.
Amen. So fall to 't: 72
Rich men sin, and I eat root.'

[*Eats and drinks.*]
Much good dich thy good heart, Apemantus!

Tim. Captain Alcibiades, your heart's in the
field now.   76

Alcib. My heart is ever at your service, my
lord.

Tim. You had rather be at a breakfast of
enemies than a dinner of friends.   80

Alcib. So they were bleeding-new, my lord,
there's no meat like 'em: I could wish my best
friend at such a feast.

Apem. Would all those flatterers were thine
enemies, then, that then thou mightst kill 'em
and bid me to 'em!   86

First Lord. Might we but have that happiness, my lord, that you would once use our
hearts, whereby we might express some part
of our zeals, we should think ourselves for ever
perfect.   91

Tim. O, no doubt, my good friends, but the
gods themselves have provided that I shall have
much help from you: how had you been my
friends else? why have you that charitable title
from thousands, did not you chiefly belong to
my heart? I have told more of you to myself
than you can with modesty speak in your own
behalf, and thus far I confirm you. O you 99

74 dich: *do it*   81 bleeding-new: *freshly killed*
91 perfect: *satisfied*   95 charitable title: *name of endearment*
96 from: *from among*

gods, think I, what need we have any friends, if
we should ne'er have need of 'em? they were the
most needless creatures living should we ne'er
have use for 'em, and would most resemble
sweet instruments hung up in cases, that keep
their sounds to themselves. Why, I have often
wished myself poorer, that I might come nearer
to you. We are born to do benefits: and what 107
better or properer can we call our own than the
riches of our friends? O, what a precious comfort 'tis, to have so many, like brothers, com-
manding one another's fortunes! O joy, e'en
made away ere 't can be born! Mine eyes cannot
hold out water, methinks: to forget their faults,
I drink to you.

Apem. Thou weep'st to make them drink,
Timon. 116
Sec. Lord. Joy had the like conception in our eyes,
And, at that instant, like a babe, sprung up.
Apem. Ho, ho! I laugh to think that babe a bastard.
Third Lord. I promise you, my lord, you mov'd me
much. 120
Apem. Much! *Sound Tucket.*
Tim. What means that trump?

Enter Servant.

How now!
Serv. Please you, my lord, there are certain
ladies most desirous of admittance. 124
Tim. Ladies! What are their wills?
Serv. There comes with them a forerunner,

111, 112 O joy . . . born; *cf. n.*
115, 116 Thou weep'st . . . Timon; *cf. n.*
118 sprung up: *stirred within us, quickened*
121 S. d. Tucket: *trumpet call*

my lord, which bears that office, to signify their
pleasures.   128
 Tim. I pray, let them be admitted.

     Enter Cupid.

 Cup. Hail to thee, worthy Timon! and to all
That of his bounties taste! The five best senses
Acknowledge thee their patron, and come freely   132
To gratulate thy plenteous bosom: th' ear,
Taste, touch, and smell, pleas'd from thy table rise;
They only now come but to feast thine eyes.
 Tim. They're welcome all; let 'em have kind ad-
  mittance: 136
Music, make their welcome!   [*Exit Cupid.*]
 First Lord. You see, my lord, how ample you're
  beloved.

[*Music.*] *Enter Cupid with the masque of Ladies
[as] Amazons, with lutes in their hands, dancing
and playing.*

 Apem. Hoy-day, what a sweep of vanity comes
  this way!
They dance! they are mad women.   140
Like madness is the glory of this life,
As this pomp shows to a little oil and root.
We make ourselves fools, to disport ourselves,
And spend our flatteries, to drink those men   144
Upon whose age we void it up again
With poisonous spite and envy.
Who lives, that's not depraved or depraves?

---

129 S. d. Enter Cupid; *cf. n.*   133 gratulate: *salute*
138 ample: *fully*   138 S. d. with . . . Amazons; *cf. n.*
139 Hoy-day: *exclamation of surprise* 140 mad women; *cf. n.*
141, 142 Like madness . . . root; *cf. n.* 145 void . . . up: *vomit*
147 depraved: *vilified* depraves: *vilifies*

Who dies, that bears not one spurn to their
    graves   148
Of their friend's gift?
I should fear those that dance before me now
Would one day stamp upon me: 't has been done;
Men shut their doors against a setting sun.   152

*The Lords rise from table, with much adoring of
Timon; and to show their loves each singles out
an Amazon, and all dance, men with women, a
lofty strain or two to the hautboys, and cease.*

  Tim. You have done our pleasures much grace, fair
    ladies,
Set a fair fashion on our entertainment,
Which was not half so beautiful and kind;
You have added worth unto 't and lustre,   156
And entertain'd me with mine own device:
I am to thank you for 't.
    First Lady. My lord, you take us even at the best.
    Apem. Faith, for the worst is filthy, and
would not hold taking, I doubt me.   161
  Tim. Ladies, there is an idle banquet
Attends you: please you to dispose yourselves.
    All Lad. Most thankfully, my lord.   164
               Exeunt [Cupid and Ladies].
  Tim. Flavius!
  Flav. My lord?
  Tim.   The little casket bring me hither.
  Flav. Yes, my lord. [*Aside.*] More jewels yet!
There is no crossing him in 's humour;   168
Else I should tell him—well, i' faith, I should—

148, 149 spurn . . . gift: *contemptuous blow received from a friend*
152 *Cf. n.*   155 kind: *gracious*
161 hold taking: *endure handling*   doubt: *fear*
162 idle: *trifling*   banquet: *dessert*   163 Attends: *which awaits*

When all's spent, he'd be cross'd then, an he could.
'Tis pity bounty had not eyes behind,
That man might ne'er be wretched for his mind.   172
                                                  Exit.

  First Lord. Where be our men?
  Serv. Here, my lord, in readiness.
  Sec. Lord. Our horses!

   Enter Flavius [with the casket].

  Tim. O, my friends! I have one word to say to
  you;   176
Look you, my good lord,
I must entreat you, honour me so much
As to advance this jewel; accept it and wear it,
Kind my lord.   180
  First Lord. I am so far already in your gifts,—
  All. So are we all.

    Enter a Servant.

  Serv. My lord, there are certain nobles of the
  senate
Newly alighted and come to visit you.   184
  Tim. They are fairly welcome.
  Flav.   I beseech your honour,
Vouchsafe me a word; it does concern you near.
  Tim. Near! why, then, another time I'll hear thee:
I prithee, let's be provided to show them entertain-
  ment.   188
  Flav. [*Aside.*] I scarce know how.

   Enter another Servant.

  Sec. Serv. May it please your honour, Lord Lucius,

170 *Cf. n.*   171, 172 'Tis pity . . . mind; *cf. n.*
172 mind: *magnanimity*
179 advance: *do honor to (by taking it into your possession)*
185 fairly: *courteously*   186 near: *intimately*   187 *Cf. n.*

Out of his free love, hath presented to you
Four milk-white horses, trapp'd in silver.   192
   Tim. I shall accept them fairly: let the presents
Be worthily entertain'd.

Enter a third Servant.

                          How now! what news?
   Third Serv. Please you, my lord, that honour-
able gentleman, Lord Lucullus, entreats your
company to-morrow to hunt with him, and has
sent your honour two brace of greyhounds.   198
   Tim. I'll hunt with him; and let them be receiv'd,
Not without fair reward.
   Flav.   [*Aside.*] What will this come to?
He commands us to provide, and give great gifts,
And all out of an empty coffer:
Nor will he know his purse, or yield me this,
To show him what a beggar his heart is,   204
Being of no power to make his wishes good.
His promises fly so beyond his state
That what he speaks is all in debt; he owes
For every word: he is so kind that he now   208
Pays interest for 't; his land's put to their books.
Well, would I were gently put out of office,
Before I were forc'd out!
Happier he that has no friend to feed   212
Than such that do e'en enemies exceed.
I bleed inwardly for my lord.   *Exit.*
   Tim.   You do yourselves
Much wrong, you bate too much of your own merits.
Here, my lord, a trifle of our love.   216
   Sec. Lord. With more than common thanks I will
     receive it.

---

194 entertain'd: *accepted*   203 yield: *grant*
213 such: *such friends*   215 bate: *deduct*

 Third Lord. O, he's the very soul of bounty!

 Tim. And now I remember, my lord, you gave
Good words the other day of a bay courser 220
I rode on. It is yours, because you lik'd it.

 Third Lord. O, I beseech you, pardon me, my lord,
  in that.

 Tim. You may take my word, my lord; I know no
  man
Can justly praise, but what he does affect: 224
I weigh my friend's affection with mine own:
I'll tell you true. I'll call to you.

 All Lords.   O, none so welcome.

 Tim. I take all and your several visitations
So kind to heart, 'tis not enough to give: 228
Methinks, I could deal kingdoms to my friends,
And ne'er be weary. Alcibiades,
Thou art a soldier, therefore seldom rich;
It comes in charity to thee: for all thy living 232
Is 'mongst the dead, and all the lands thou hast
Lie in a pitch'd field.

 Alcib.   Ay, defil'd land, my lord.

 First Lord. We are so virtuously bound—

 Tim.   And so
Am I to you.

 Sec. Lord. So infinitely endear'd,— 236

 Tim. All to you. Lights, more lights!

 First Lord.   The best of happiness,
Honour, and fortunes, keep with you, Lord Timon!

 Tim. Ready for his friends.

           Exeunt Lords.

 Apem.   What a coil's here!
Serving of becks and jutting-out of bums! 240

226 I'll call to you; *cf. n.*   227 visitations: *visits*
234 defil'd; *cf. n.*   235 bound: *under obligation*
239 coil: *fuss* 240 *Offering of obeisances and excessive bowing*

I doubt whether their legs be worth the sums
That are given for 'em. Friendship's full of dregs:
Methinks, false hearts should never have sound legs.
Thus honest fools lay out their wealth on court'-
    sies.   244

    Tim. Now, Apemantus, if thou wert not sullen,
I would be good to thee.

    Apem. No, I'll nothing: for if I should be
bribed too, there would be none left to rail upon
thee; and then thou wouldst sin the faster. Thou
givest so long, Timon, I fear me thou wilt give
away thyself in paper shortly: what needs these
feasts, pomps, and vain-glories?   252

    Tim. Nay, an you begin to rail on society
once, I am sworn not to give regard to you.
Farewell; and come with better music.   *Exit.*

    Apem. So: 256
Thou wilt not hear me now; thou shalt not then;
I'll lock thy heaven from thee.
O, that men's ears should be
To counsel deaf, but not to flattery!   *Exit.*

ACT SECOND

Scene One

[*Athens. A Room in a Senator's House*]

Enter a Senator [with papers in his hand].

    Sen. And late five thousand: to Varro and to Isi-
    dore
He owes nine thousand; besides my former sum,

241 legs: *cf. n.*   251 paper: *bonds*   255 come . . . music; *cf. n.*
258 heaven: *salvation, good advice*   1 late: *lately*

Which makes it five and twenty. Still in motion
Of raging waste? It cannot hold; it will not.   4
If I want gold, steal but a beggar's dog
And give it Timon, why, the dog coins gold:
If I would sell my horse and buy twenty moe
Better than he, why, give my horse to Timon;   8
Ask nothing, give it him, it foals me, straight,
And able horses. No porter at his gate,
But rather one that smiles and still invites
All that pass by. It cannot hold; no reason   12
Can found his state in safety. Caphis, ho!
Caphis, I say!

Enter Caphis.

Caph.   Here, sir; what is your pleasure?
Sen. Get on your cloak, and haste you to Lord
    Timon;
Importune him for my moneys; be not ceas'd   16
With slight denial; nor then silenc'd, when—
'Commend me to your master'—and the cap
Plays in the right hand, thus: but tell him,
My uses cry to me, I must serve my turn   20
Out of mine own; his days and times are past,
And my reliances on his fracted dates
Have smit my credit: I love and honour him,
But must not break my back to heal his finger: 24
Immediate are my needs; and my relief
Must not be toss'd and turn'd to me in words,
But find supply immediate. Get you gone:
Put on a most importunate aspect,   28
A visage of demand; for, I do fear,
When every feather sticks in his own wing,

10 No porter, etc.; *cf. n.*   11 still: *always*   12 hold: *continue*
16 be not ceas'd: *do not allow yourself to be silenced*
20 uses: *needs*   22 fracted: *broken*   26 turn'd: *flung back*
30 his: *its (that of the bird to which it belongs)*; *cf. n.*

Lord Timon will be left a naked gull,
Which flashes now a phœnix. Get you gone.   32
   Caph. I go, sir.
   Sen. 'I go, sir!' Take the bonds along with you,
And have the dates in compt.
   Caph.   I will, sir.
   Sen.   Go.
                             Exeunt.

Scene Two

[*The Same. A Hall in Timon's House*]

Enter Steward [*Flavius*] *with many bills in his hand.*

   Flav. No care, no stop! so senseless of expense,
That he will neither know how to maintain it,
Nor cease his flow of riot: takes no account
How things go from him; nor resumes no care   4
Of what is to continue: never mind
Was to be so unwise, to be so kind.
What shall be done? He will not hear, till feel:
I must be round with him, now he comes from hunt-
    ing.   8
Fie, fie, fie, fie!

Enter Caphis, [*and the Servants of*] *Isidore and
Varro.*

   Caph.   Good even, Varro. What,
You come for money?
   Var. Serv.   Is 't not your business too?
   Caph. It is: and yours too, Isidore?
   Isid. Serv.   It is so.

35 compt: *reckoning, for the calculation of interest due*
4 resumes: *takes*   5, 6 never mind, etc.; *cf. n.*
7 hear, till feel: *listen to warnings till the actual disaster befalls him*
8 round: *plain*   9, 11 Varro . . . Isidore; *cf. n.*

Caph. Would we were all discharged!

Var. Serv. I fear it. 12

Caph. Here comes the lord!

Enter Timon, and his Train [Alcibiades, Lords, and Others].

Tim. So soon as dinner's done, we'll forth again,
My Alcibiades. With me? what is your will?

Caph. My lord, here is a note of certain dues. 16

Tim. Dues! Whence are you?

Caph. Of Athens here, my lord.

Tim. Go to my steward.

Caph. Please it your lordship, he hath put me off
To the succession of new days this month: 20
My master is awak'd by great occasion
To call upon his own, and humbly prays you
That with your other noble parts you'll suit
In giving him his right.

Tim. Mine honest friend, 24
I prithee but repair to me next morning.

Caph. Nay, good my lord,—

Tim. Contain thyself, good friend.

Var. Serv. One Varro's servant, my good lord,—

Isid. Serv. From Isidore;
He humbly prays your speedy payment. 28

Caph. If you did know, my lord, my master's
wants,—

Var. Serv. 'Twas due on forfeiture, my lord, six
weeks
And past.

Isid. Serv. Your steward puts me off, my lord; 32

12 discharged: *paid*   14 we'll forth again; *cf. n.*
20 To the succession of new days: *from one day to another*
21 occasion: *particular need*
23 parts: *endowments*   suit: *be consistent*
25 but: *only*   repair: *return*

And I am sent expressly to your lordship.
  Tim. Give me breath.
I do beseech you, good my lords, keep on;
I'll wait upon you instantly.

                    [*Exeunt Alcibiades and Lords.*]
          [*To Flavius.*] Come hither: pray you, 36
How goes the world, that I am thus encounter'd
With clamorous demands of date-broke bonds,
And the detention of long-since-due debts,
Against my honour?
  Flav.   Please you, gentlemen,   40
The time is unagreeable to this business:
Your importunacy cease till after dinner,
That I may make his lordship understand
Wherefore you are not paid.
  Tim.   Do so, my friends. 44
See them well entertained.   [*Exit.*]
  Flav.   Pray, draw near.   *Exit.*

          Enter Apemantus and Fool.

  Caph. Stay, stay, here comes the fool with
Apemantus: let's ha' some sport with 'em.
  Var. Serv. Hang him, he'll abuse us.   48
  Isid. Serv. A plague upon him, dog!
  Var. Serv. How dost, fool?
  Apem. Dost dialogue with thy shadow?
  Var. Serv. I speak not to thee.   52
  Apem. No, 'tis to thyself.   [*To the Fool.*]
Come away.
  Isid. Serv. [*To Var. Serv.*] There's   the   fool
hangs on your back already.   56
  Apem. No, thou stand'st single; thou'rt not on him
    yet.

---

38 date-broke: *overdue*   41 unagreeable: *unsuitable*
57 No, thou . . . yet; *cf. n.*

Caph. Where's the fool now?

Apem. He last asked the question. Poor
rogues, and usurers' men! bawds between gold
and want!   61

All Serv. What are we, Apemantus?

Apem. Asses.

All Serv. Why?   64

Apem. That you ask me what you are, and do
not know yourselves. Speak to 'em, fool.

Fool. How do you, gentlemen?

All Serv. Gramercies, good fool: how does
your mistress?   69

Fool. She's e'en setting on water to scald
such chickens as you are. Would we could see
you at Corinth!   72

Apem. Good! gramercy.

Enter Page.

Fool. Look you, here comes my mistress'
page.

Page. [*To the Fool.*] Why, how now, captain!
what do you in this wise company? How dost
thou, Apemantus?

Apem. Would I had a rod in my mouth, that
I might answer thee profitably.   80

Page. Prithee, Apemantus, read me the
superscription of these letters: I know not
which is which.

Apem. Canst not read?   84

Page. No.

Apem. There will little learning die then,
that day thou art hanged. This is to Lord

59 He: *he who*   68 Gramercies: *God-a-mercy, God reward you*
72 Corinth: (*allusively*) *house of ill fame*
76 captain: *a familiar term of address*

Timon; this to Alcibiades. Go; thou wast born
a bastard, and thou'lt die a bawd.   89

Page. Thou wast whelped a dog, and thou
shalt famish,—a dog's death. Answer not; I am
gone.   *Exit.*

Apem. E'en so thou outrunn'st grace.
Fool, I will go with you to Lord Timon's.

Fool. Will you leave me there?

Apem. If Timon stay at home. You three
serve three usurers?   97

All Serv. Ay; would they served us!

Apem. So would I,—as good a trick as ever
hangman served thief.   100

Fool. Are you three usurers' men?

All Serv. Ay, fool.

Fool. I think no usurer but has a fool to his
servant: my mistress is one, and I am her fool.
When men come to borrow of your masters,
they approach sadly, and go away merry; but
they enter my mistress' house merrily, and go
away sadly: the reason of this?   108

Var. Serv. I could render one.

Apem. Do it, then, that we may account thee
a whoremaster and a knave; which notwith-
standing, thou shalt be no less esteemed.   112

Var. Serv. What is a whoremaster, fool?

Fool. A fool in good clothes, and something
like thee. 'Tis a spirit: sometime 't appears
like a lord; sometime like a lawyer; sometime
like a philosopher, with two stones moe than 's
artificial one. He is very often like a knight;
and generally, in all shapes that man goes up

94 to Lord Timon's; *cf. n.*   115 sometime: *at times*
117 philosopher, etc.; *cf. n.*

and down in from fourscore to thirteen, this
spirit walks in.   121

   Var. Serv. Thou art not altogether a fool.

   Fool. Nor thou altogether a wise man: as
much foolery as I have, so much wit thou
lack'st.   125

   Apem. That answer might have become Apemantus.

   All Serv. Aside, aside; here comes Lord
Timon.   129

       Enter Timon and Steward [Flavius].

   Apem. Come with me, fool, come.

   Fool. I do not always follow lover, elder
brother, and woman; sometime the philosopher.
             [Exeunt Apemantus and Fool.]

   Flav. Pray you, walk near: I'll speak with you
anon.   *Exeunt [Servants].*

   Tim. You make me marvel; wherefore, ere this
time,

Had you not fully laid my state before me,

That I might so have rated my expense   136

As I had leave of means?

   Flav.   You would not hear me,

At many leisures I propos'd.

   Tim.   Go to:

Perchance some single vantages you took,

When my indisposition put you back;   140

And that unaptness made your minister,

Thus to excuse yourself.

   Flav.   O my good lord,

At many times I brought in my accounts,

136 rated: *allotted*   137 As . . . means: *as my means permitted*
138 propos'd: *spoke*   139 vantages: *opportunities*
140 indisposition: *disinclination*
141 *And made that disinclination your agent*

Laid them before you; you would throw them off, 144
And say, you found them in mine honesty.
When for some trifling present you have bid me
Return so much, I have shook my head and wept;
Yea, 'gainst the authority of manners, pray'd you 148
To hold your hand more close: I did endure
Not seldom, nor no slight checks, when I have
Prompted you in the ebb of your estate
And your great flow of debts. My loved lord, 152
Though you hear now, too late!—yet now's a time—
The greatest of your having lacks a half
To pay your present debts.
  Tim.   Let all my land be sold.
  Flav. 'Tis all engag'd, some forfeited and gone, 156
And what remains will hardly stop the mouth
Of present dues: the future comes apace:
What shall defend the interim? and at length
How goes our reckoning? 160
  Tim. To Lacedæmon did my land extend.
  Flav. O my good lord, the world is but a word:
Were it all yours to give it in a breath,
How quickly were it gone!
  Tim.   You tell me true. 164
  Flav. If you suspect my husbandry or falsehood,
Call me before the exactest auditors,
And set me on the proof. So the gods bless me,
When all our offices have been oppress'd 168
With riotous feeders, when our vaults have wept
With drunken spilth of wine, when every room
Hath blaz'd with lights and bray'd with minstrelsy,

151 Prompted . . . in: *reminded . . . of*
153 yet now's a time; *cf. n.*
154 *The most you have is but half enough*
165 husbandry: *management; cf. n.*
167 set me on: *put me to* proof: *test*
168 offices: *parts of house-buildings devoted to purely household matters* 170 spilth: *spilling*

I have retir'd me to a wasteful cock,   172
And set mine eyes at flow.
    Tim.   Prithee, no more.
    Flav. Heavens, have I said, the bounty of this
      lord!
How many prodigal bits have slaves and peasants
This night englutted! Who is not Timon's?   176
What heart, head, sword, force, means, but is Lord
      Timon's?
Great Timon, noble, worthy, royal Timon!
Ah, when the means are gone that buy this praise,
The breath is gone whereof this praise is made: 180
Feast-won, fast-lost; one cloud of winter showers,
These flies are couch'd.
    Tim.   Come, sermon me no further:
No villainous bounty yet hath pass'd my heart;
Unwisely, not ignobly, have I given.   184
Why dost thou weep? Canst thou the conscience lack,
To think I shall lack friends? Secure thy heart;
If I would broach the vessels of my love,
And try the argument of hearts by borrowing,   188
Men and men's fortunes could I frankly use
As I can bid thee speak.
    Flav.   Assurance bless your thoughts.
    Tim. And in some sort these wants of mine are
      crown'd,
That I account them blessings; for by these   192
Shall I try friends: you shall perceive how you
Mistake my fortunes; I am wealthy in my friends.
Within there! Flaminius! Servilius!

---

175 bits: *portions*   176 englutted: *swallowed up*
182 are couch'd: *go into hiding*   186 Secure: *set at ease*
188 argument: *summary of subject-matter of a book, (figuratively)*
    contents   189 frankly: *freely*
190 Assurance bless: *may the actual fact justify*
191 crown'd: *glorified*

Enter three Servants.

Serv. My lord? my lord?   196

Tim. I will dispatch you severally: you, to
Lord Lucius: to Lord Lucullus you: I hunted
with his honour to-day; you, to Sempronius:
Commend me to their loves; and, I am proud,
say, that my occasions have found time to use
'em toward a supply of money: let the request
be fifty talents.

Flam. As you have said, my lord.   204

Flav. [*Aside.*] Lord Lucius, and Lucullus? hum!

Tim. [*To another Servant.*] Go you, sir, to the sen-
ators—
Of whom, even to the state's best health, I have
Deserv'd this hearing—bid 'em send o' the in-
stant   208
A thousand talents to me.

Flav.   I have been bold,
For that I knew it the most general way,
To them to use your signet and your name,
But they do shake their heads, and I am here   212
No richer in return.

Tim.   Is 't true? can 't be?

Flav. They answer, in a joint and corporate voice,
That now they are at fall, want treasure, cannot
Do what they would; are sorry—you are honour-
able,—   216
But yet they could have wish'd—they know not—
Something hath been amiss—a noble nature
May catch a wrench—would all were well—'tis
pity:—

197 severally: *separately*   207, 208 Of whom . . . hearing; *cf. n.*
208 o' the instant: *immediately*
214 corporate: *belonging to a body of persons*
215 at fall: *at a low ebb*

And so, intending other serious matters,   220
After distasteful looks and these hard fractions,
With certain half-caps and cold-moving nods
They froze me into silence.
    Tim.   You gods, reward them!
Prithee, man, look cheerly. These old fellows   224
Have their ingratitude in them hereditary:
Their blood is cak'd, 'tis cold, it seldom flows;
'Tis lack of kindly warmth they are not kind;
And nature, as it grows again toward earth,   228
Is fashion'd for the journey, dull and heavy.
[*To a Servant.*] Go to Ventidius. [*To Flavius.*]
    Prithee, be not sad;
Thou art true and honest; ingeniously I speak,
No blame belongs to thee. [*To Servant.*] Ventidius
    lately   232
Buried his father, by whose death he's stepp'd
Into a great estate: when he was poor,
Imprison'd, and in scarcity of friends,
I clear'd him with five talents: greet   from
    me;   236
Bid him suppose some good necessity
Touches his friend, which craves to be remember'd
With those five talents. [*Exit Servant. To Flavius.*]
    That had, give 't these fellows
To whom 'tis instant due. Ne'er speak, or think   240
That Timon's fortunes 'mong his friends can sink.
    Flav. I would I could not think it: that thought is
    bounty's foe;
Being free itself, it thinks all others so.   *Exeunt.*

220 intending: *pretending*   221 fractions: *fragments*
222 half-caps: *half-courteous salutes*   cold-moving: *frigid*
231 ingeniously: *ingenuously*   240 instant: *immediately*
243 free: *liberal*

ACT THIRD

Scene One

[Athens. A Room in Lucullus's House]

Flaminius waiting to speak with a Lord [Lucullus] from his master, enters a servant to him.

Serv. I have told my lord of you; he is coming down to you.
Flam. I thank you, sir.

Enter Lucullus.

Serv. Here's my lord.   4
Lucul. [*Aside.*] One of Lord Timon's men? a
gift, I warrant. Why, this hits right; I dreamt
of a silver basin and ewer to-night. Flaminius,
honest Flaminius; you are very respectively wel-   8
come, sir. Fill me some wine. [*Exit Servant.*]
And how does that honourable, complete, free-
hearted gentleman of Athens, thy very bountiful
good lord and master?   12
Flam. His health is well, sir.
Lucul. I am right glad that his health is well,
sir: and what hast thou there under thy cloak,
pretty Flaminius?   16
Flam. Faith, nothing but an empty box, sir;
which, in my lord's behalf, I come to entreat
your honour to supply; who, having great and
instant occasion to use fifty talents, hath sent to
your lordship to furnish him, nothing doubting
your present assistance therein.   22
Lucul. La, la, la, la! 'nothing doubting,' says

8 respectively: *particularly*   10 complete: *accomplished*

he? Alas, good lord! a noble gentleman 'tis, if
he would not keep so good a house. Many a
time and often I ha' dined with him, and told
him on 't; and come again to supper to him, of
purpose to have him spend less; and yet he
would embrace no counsel, take no warning by
my coming. Every man has his fault, and
honesty is his: I ha' told him on 't, but I could
ne'er get him from 't.   32

Enter Servant with Wine.

Serv. Please your lordship, here is the wine.
Lucul. Flaminius, I have noted thee always
wise. Here's to thee.
Flam. Your lordship speaks your pleasure.   36
Lucul. I have observed thee always for a
towardly, prompt spirit—give thee thy due—and
one that knows what belongs to reason; and
canst use the time well, if the time use thee well:
good parts in thee. [*To the Servant.*] Get you
gone, sirrah. [*Exit Servant.*] Draw nearer, 42
honest Flaminius. Thy lord's a bountiful gentleman: but thou art wise; and thou knowest well
enough, although thou comest to me, that this
is no time to lend money, especially upon bare
friendship, without security. Here's three solidares for thee: good boy, wink at me, and say
thou saw'st me not. Fare thee well.   49
Flam. Is 't possible the world should so much
    differ,
And we alive that liv'd? Fly, damned baseness,

---

31 honesty: *generosity*   38 towardly: *docile*
47 solidares: *small coins, shillings* (?)
48 wink at: *seem not to see*   51 And we alive that liv'd; *cf. n.*

To him that worships thee!   52
> [*Throwing back the money.*]

Lucul. Ha! now I see thou art a fool, and fit
for thy master.   *Exit Lucullus.*

Flam. May these add to the number that may scald
thee!

Let molten coin be thy damnation,   56
Thou disease of a friend, and not himself!
Has friendship such a faint and milky heart,
It turns in less than two nights? O you gods,
I feel my master's passion! This slave, unto his
honour,   60
Has my lord's meat in him:
Why should it thrive and turn to nutriment,
When he is turn'd to poison?
O, may diseases only work upon 't!   64
And, when he's sick to death, let not that part of
nature
Which my lord paid for, be of any power
To expel sickness, but prolong his hour!   *Exit.*

Scene Two

[*The Same. A Public Place*]

Enter Lucius, with three Strangers.

Luc. Who, the Lord Timon? he is my very
good friend, and an honourable gentleman.

First Stran. We know him for no less, though
we are but strangers to him. But I can tell you
one thing, my lord, and which I hear from
common rumours: now Lord Timon's happy
hours are done and past, and his estate shrinks
from him.   8

---

56 molten coin; *cf. n.*   60 passion: *violent emotion*

Luc. Fie, no, do not believe it; he cannot
want for money.

Sec. Stran. But believe you this, my lord,
that, not long ago one of his men was with the
Lord Lucullus to borrow so many talents; nay,
urged extremely for 't, and showed what necessity belonged to 't, and yet was denied.

Luc. How!   16

Sec. Stran. I tell you, denied, my lord.

Luc. What a strange case was that! now, before the gods, I am ashamed on 't. Denied that
honourable man! there was very little honour
showed in 't. For my own part, I must needs
confess, I have received some small kindnesses
from him, as money, plate, jewels, and such like
trifles, nothing comparing to his; yet, had he
mistook him and sent to me, I should ne'er have
denied his occasion so many talents.   26

Enter Servilius.

Servil. See, by good hap, yonder's my lord;
I have sweat to see his honour. My honoured
lord!

Luc. Servilius! you are kindly met, sir.
Fare thee well: commend me to thy honourable
virtuous lord, my very exquisite friend. [*Going.*] 22

Servil. May it please your honour, my lord
hath sent—

Luc. Ha! what has he sent? I am so much
endeared to that lord; he's ever sending: how
shall I thank him, thinkest thou? And what
has he sent now?   38

25 mistook: *misdoubted* (?)   26 occasion: *necessity*
27 hap: *fortune*

Servil. He has only sent his present occasion now, my lord; requesting your lordship to supply his instant use with so many talents. 41

Luc. I know his lordship is but merry with me; He cannot want fifty-five hundred talents.

Servil. But in the mean time he wants less, my lord. 44

If his occasion were not virtuous, I should not urge it half so faithfully.

Luc. Dost thou speak seriously, Servilius?

Servil. Upon my soul, 'tis true, sir. 48

Luc. What a wicked beast was I to disfurnish myself against such a good time, when I might ha' shown myself honourable! how unluckily it happened, that I should purchase the day before for a little part, and undo a great deal of honour! Servilius, now, before the gods, I am not able to do—the more beast, I say:—I was sending to use Lord Timon myself, these gentlemen can witness; but I would not, for the wealth of Athens, I had done 't now. Commend me bountifully to his good lordship; and I hope his honour will conceive the fairest of me, because I 60 have no power to be kind: and tell him this from me, I count it one of my greatest afflictions, say, that I cannot pleasure such an honourable gentleman. Good Servilius, will you befriend me so far as to use mine own words to him? 66

Servil. Yes, sir, I shall.

Luc. I'll look you out a good turn, Servilius.

Exit Servilius.

---

45 virtuous: *forcible*   49 disfurnish: *deprive*
50 against: *on the eve of*   52-54 that I . . . honour; *cf. n.*
60 conceive . . . fairest: *make the most favorable judgment*

True, as you said, Timon is shrunk indeed;
And he that's once denied will hardly speed.   *Exit.*
 First Stran. Do you observe this, Hostilius?
 Sec. Stran.   Ay, too well.
 First Stran. Why this is the world's soul; and just
  of the same piece   72
Is every flatterer's spirit.   Who can call him
His friend that dips in the same dish? for, in
My knowing, Timon has been this lord's father,
And kept his credit with his purse;   76
Supported his estate; nay, Timon's money
Has paid his men their wages: he ne'er drinks
But Timon's silver treads upon his lip;
And yet—O, see the monstrousness of man   80
When he looks out in an ungrateful shape!—
He does deny him, in respect of his,
What charitable men afford to beggars.
 Third Stran. Religion groans at it.
 First Stran.   For mine own part,   84
I never tasted Timon in my life,
Nor came any of his bounties over me,
To mark me for his friend; yet, I protest,
For his right noble mind, illustrious virtue,   88
And honourable carriage,
Had his necessity made use of me,
I would have put my wealth into donation,
And the best half should have return'd to him,   92
So much I love his heart.   But, I perceive,
Men must learn now with pity to dispense;
For policy sits above conscience.   *Exeunt.*

70 speed: *be successful*
82 in respect of his: *in comparison with his own resources*
84 Religion: *proper feeling*
85 tasted: *had experience of the qualities of*

Scene Three

[*The Same. A Room in Sempronius's House*]

*Enter a third servant [of Timon's] with Sempronius,
another of Timon's friends.*

Sem. Must he needs trouble me in 't,—hum! 'bove
all others?
He might have tried Lord Lucius, or Lucullus;
And now Ventidius is wealthy too,
Whom he redeem'd from prison: all these   4
Owe their estates unto him.
Serv.   My lord,
They have all been touch'd and found base metal, for
They have all denied him.
Sem.   How! have they denied him?
Have Ventidius and Lucullus denied him?   8
And does he send to me? Three? hum!
It shows but little love or judgment in him:
Must I be his last refuge? His friends, like physi-
cians,
Thrice give him over: must I take the cure upon
me?   12
He has much disgrac'd me in 't; I'm angry at him,
That might have known my place: I see no sense for 't,
But his occasions might have woo'd me first;
For, in my conscience, I was the first man   16
That e'er received gift from him:
And does he think so backwardly of me now,
That I'll requite it last? No.
So it may prove an argument of laughter   20
To the rest, and 'mongst lords I be thought a fool.
I'd rather than the worth of thrice the sum,

6 touch'd: *tested as with the touchstone*   12 Thrice: *cf. n.*
18 backwardly: *perversely*   20 argument: *theme*

He'd sent to me first, but for my mind's sake;
I'd such a courage to do him good. But now re-
    turn,   24
And with their faint reply this answer join;
Who bates mine honour shall not know my coin.
                             Exit.

    Serv. Excellent! Your lordship's a goodly
villain. The devil knew not what he did when
he made man politic; he crossed himself by 't:
and I cannot think but in the end the villainies 30
of man will set him clear. How fairly this lord
strives to appear foul! takes virtuous copies to
be wicked; like those that under hot ardent zeal
would set whole realms on fire:
Of such a nature is his politic love.
This was my lord's best hope; now all are fled   36
Save only the gods. Now his friends are dead,
Doors, that were ne'er acquainted with their wards
Many a bounteous year, must be employ'd
Now to guard sure their master;   40
And this is all a liberal course allows;
Who cannot keep his wealth must keep his house.
                             Exit.

Scene Four

[*The Same. A Hall in Timon's House*]

*Enter Varro's man [men] meeting others. All
Timon's creditors to wait for his coming out.
Then enter [servant of] Lucius and Hortensius.*

    First Var. Serv. Well met; good morrow, Titus
and Hortensius.

24 courage: *inclination*   25 faint: *timid*
28-31 The devil . . . clear; *cf. n.*
31 set . . . clear: *place in an innocent light*   32 copies: *models*
38 wards: *bars*   40 sure: *in safety*
42 keep . . . house: *remain within doors*

Tit. The like to you, kind Varro.

Hor.   Lucius!
What, do we meet together?

Luc. Serv.   Ay, and I think
One business does command us all; for mine   4
Is money.

Tit. So is theirs and ours.

Enter Philotus.

Luc. Serv.   And Sir Philotus too!

Phi. Good day at once.

Luc. Serv.   Welcome, good brother.
What do you think the hour?

Phi.   Labouring for nine.   8

Luc. Serv. So much?

Phi.   Is not my lord seen yet?

Luc. Serv.   Not yet.

Phi. I wonder on 't; he was wont to shine at seven.

Luc. Serv. Ay, but the days are waxed shorter with
    him:
You must consider that a prodigal course   12
Is like the sun's; but not, like his, recoverable.
I fear,
'Tis deepest winter in Lord Timon's purse;
That is, one may reach deep enough and yet   16
Find little.

Phi.   I am of your fear for that.

Tit. I'll show you how to observe a strange event.
Your lord sends now for money.

Hor.   Most true, he does.

Tit. And he wears jewels now of Timon's gift,   20
For which I wait for money.

Hor. It is against my heart.

7 at once: *to all of you together*
13 Is like the sun's; *cf. n.*   recoverable: *capable of being retraced*

 Luc. Serv.   Mark, how strange it shows,
Timon in this should pay more than he owes:
And e'en as if your lord should wear rich jewels, 24
And send for money for 'em.
 Hor. I'm weary of this charge, the gods can wit-
ness:
I know my lord hath spent of Timon's wealth,
And now ingratitude makes it worse than stealth. 28
 First Var. Serv. Yes, mine's three thousand crowns:
  what's yours?
 Luc. Serv. Five thousand mine.
 First Var. Serv. 'Tis much deep; and it should
  seem by the sum,
Your master's confidence was above mine; 32
Else, surely, his had equall'd.

     Enter Flaminius.

 Tit. One of Lord Timon's men.
 Luc. Serv. Flaminius! Sir, a word. Pray, is
my lord ready to come forth? 36
 Flam. No, indeed he is not.
 Tit. We attend his lordship: pray, signify so
much.
 Flam. I need not tell him that; he knows
you are too diligent.   [*Exit Flaminius.*]
  Enter Steward [*Flavius*] *in a cloak, muffled.*
 Luc. Serv. Ha! is not that his steward muffled so?
He goes away in a cloud: call him, call him.
 Tit. Do you hear, sir? 44
 Sec. Var. Serv. By your leave, sir.
 Flav. What do ye ask of me, my friend?
 Tit. We wait for certain money here, sir.
 Flav.   Ay,
If money were as certain as your waiting, 48

23 shows: *appears*   26 charge: *commission*

'Twere sure enough.
Why then preferr'd you not your sums and bills,
When your false masters eat of my lord's meat?
Then they could smile and fawn upon his debts,   52
And take down the interest into their gluttonous
    maws.
You do yourselves but wrong to stir me up;
Let me pass quietly:
Believe 't, my lord and I have made an end;   56
I have no more to reckon, he to spend.
 Luc. Serv. Ay, but this answer will not serve.
 Flav. If 'twill not serve, 'tis not so base as you;
For you serve knaves.   [*Exit.*]
  First Var. Serv. How! what does his cash-
iered worship mutter?   62
  Sec. Var. Serv. No matter what; he's poor,
and that's revenge enough. Who can speak
broader than he that has no house to put his
head in? such may rail against great buildings.

Enter Servilius.

 Tit. O, here's Servilius; now we shall know
some answer.   68
 Servil. If I might beseech you, gentlemen, to
repair some other hour, I should derive much
from 't; for, take 't of my soul, my lord leans
wondrously to discontent. His comfortable
temper has forsook him; he's much out of
health, and keeps his chamber.
 Luc. Serv. Many do keep their chambers are not
sick:
And, if it be so far beyond his health,   76
Methinks he should the sooner pay his debts,
And make a clear way to the gods.

Servil.   Good gods!

Tit. We cannot take this for answer, sir.

Flam. Within. Servilius, help! my lord! my
  lord!   80

  Enter Timon, in a rage [Flaminius following].

Tim. What! are my doors oppos'd against my passage?

Have I been ever free, and must my house

Be my retentive enemy, my gaol?

The place which I have feasted, does it now,   84

Like all mankind, show me an iron heart?

Luc. Serv. Put in now, Titus.

Tit. My lord, here is my bill.

Luc. Serv. Here's mine.   88

Hor. And mine, my lord.

Both Var. Serv. And ours, my lord.

Phi. All our bills.

Tim. Knock me down with 'em: cleave me to the
  girdle.   92

Luc. Serv. Alas, my lord,—

Tim. Cut my heart in sums.

Tit. Mine, fifty talents.

Tim. Tell out my blood.   96

Luc. Serv. Five thousand crowns, my lord.

Tim. Five thousand drops pays that. What
  yours?—and yours?

First Var. Serv. My lord,—

Sec. Var. Serv. My lord,—   100

Tim. Tear me, take me; and the gods fall upon
  you!   *Exit Timon.*

  Hor. Faith, I perceive our masters may
throw their caps at their money: these debts

---

83 retentive: *confining*   86 Put in: *advance a claim*
92 Knock me down with 'em; *cf. n.*
103 throw their caps at: *give up for lost*

may well be called desperate ones, for a madman owes 'em.   *Exeunt.*

Enter Timon [and Flavius].

Tim. They have e'en put my breath from me, the
  slaves.
Creditors? devils!
  Flav. My dear lord,—   108
  Tim. What if it should be so?
  Flav. My lord,—
  Tim. I'll have it so. My steward!
  Flav. Here, my lord.   112
  Tim. So fitly? Go, bid all my friends again,
Lucius, Lucullus, and Sempronius: all:
I'll once more feast the rascals.
  Flav.   O my lord,
You only speak from your distracted soul;   116
There is not so much left to furnish out
A moderate table.
  Tim.   Be 't not in thy care: go.
I charge thee, invite them all: let in the tide
Of knaves once more; my cook and I'll provide.
                                            Exeunt.

Scene Five

[*The Same. The Senate House. The Senate
sitting.*]

*Enter three Senators at one door, Alcibiades meeting
them [later], with attendants.*

First Sen. My lord, you have my voice to it; the
  fault's
Bloody; 'tis necessary he should die;

105 S. d.; *Cf. n.*   113 fitly: *at a fitting time*
114 Sempronius: all; *cf. n.*   117 to: *as to*   1 voice: *vote*

Nothing emboldens sin so much as mercy.
    Sec. Sen. Most true; the law shall bruise him.   4
    Alcib. Honour, health, and compassion to the sen-
    ate!
    First Sen. Now, captain?
    Alcib. I am a humble suitor to your virtues;
For pity is the virtue of the law,   8
And none but tyrants use it cruelly.
It pleases time and fortune to lie heavy
Upon a friend of mine, who in hot blood
Hath stepp'd into the law, which is past depth   12
To those that without heed do plunge into 't.
He is a man, setting his fate aside,
Of comely virtues:
Nor did he soil the fact with cowardice—   16
An honour in him which buys out his fault—
But, with a noble fury and fair spirit,
Seeing his reputation touch'd to death,
He did oppose his foe: 20
And with such sober and unnoted passion
He did behave his anger, ere 'twas spent,
As if he had but prov'd an argument.
    First Sen. You undergo too strict a paradox,   24
Striving to make an ugly deed look fair:
Your words have took such pains as if they labour'd
To bring manslaughter into form, and set quarrelling
Upon the head of valour; which indeed   28
Is valour misbegot and came into the world
When sects and factions were newly born.
He's truly valiant that can wisely suffer
The worst that man can breathe, and make his
    wrongs   32

16 fact: *deed*   19 touch'd: *wounded*
21 unnoted: *undemonstrative* (?)   22 behave: *control*
24 undergo: *undertake*

His outsides, to wear them like his raiment, care-
    lessly,
And ne'er prefer his injuries to his heart,
To bring it into danger.
If wrongs be evils and enforce us kill,   36
What folly 'tis to hazard life for ill!
   Alcib. My lord,—
   First Sen. You cannot make gross sins look clear:
To revenge is no valour, but to bear.   40
   Alcib. My lords, then, under favour, pardon me,
If I speak like a captain.
Why do fond men expose themselves to battle,
And not endure all threats? sleep upon 't,   44
And let the foes quietly cut their throats,
Without repugnancy? If there be
Such valour in the bearing, what make we
Abroad? why then, women are more valiant   48
That stay at home, if bearing carry it;
And the ass more captain than the lion, the fellow
Loaden with irons wiser than the judge,
If wisdom be in suffering. O my lords,   52
As you are great, be pitifully good:
Who cannot condemn rashness in cold blood?
To kill, I grant, is sin's extremest gust;
But, in defence, by mercy, 'tis most just.   56
To be in anger is impiety;
But who is man that is not angry?
Weigh but the crime with this.
   Sec. Sen. You breathe in vain.
   Alcib.   In vain! his service done   60

34 prefer: *show*   39 clear: *unspotted*
40 *Valor consists not in revenge but in patience*
46 repugnancy: *opposition*   47 make: *do*
49 if bearing carry it; *cf. n.*   50 fellow; *cf. n.*
56 by mercy: *by a merciful condition* (?), *by your leave* (?)
60 breathe in vain: *waste your breath*

At Lacedæmon and Byzantium
Were a sufficient briber for his life.
    First Sen. What's that?
    Alcib. I say, my lords, he has done fair service,   64
And slain in fight many of your enemies:
How full of valour did he bear himself
In the last conflict, and made plenteous wounds!
    Sec. Sen. He has made too much plenty with
      'em;   68
He's a sworn rioter; he has a sin that often
Drowns him and takes his valour prisoner:
If there were no foes, that were enough
To overcome him: in that beastly fury   72
He has been known to commit outrages
And cherish factions: 'tis inferr'd to us,
His days are foul and his drink dangerous.
    First Sen. He dies.   76
    Alcib. Hard fate! he might have died in war.
My lords, if not for any parts in him—
Though his right arm might purchase his own time,
And be in debt to none—yet, more to move you,   80
Take my deserts to his and join 'em both:
And, for I know your reverend ages love
Security, I'll pawn my victories, all
My honour to you, upon his good returns.   84
If by this crime he owes the law his life,
Why, let the war receive 't in valiant gore;
For law is strict, and war is nothing more.
    First Sen. We are for law: he dies; urge it no
      more,   88
On height of our displeasure: friend or brother,
He forfeits his own blood that spills another.

62 briber: *advocate*
74 factions: *factious intrigue*   inferr'd: *alleged*
82 for: *because*
                          90 spills: *destroys*

Alcib. Must it be so? it must not be.   My lords,
I do beseech you, know me.   92
    Sec. Sen. How!
    Alcib. Call me to your remembrances.
    Third Sen.   What!
    Alcib. I cannot think but your age has forgot me;
It could not else be I should prove so base   96
To sue, and be denied such common grace:
My wounds ache at you.
    First Sen.   Do you dare our anger?
'Tis in few words, but spacious in effect;
We banish thee for ever.
    Alcib.   Banish me!   100
Banish your dotage; banish usury,
That makes the senate ugly.
    First Sen. If, after two days' shine, Athens contain
    thee,
Attend our weightier judgment.   And, not to swell
    our spirit,   104
He shall be executed presently.   *Exeunt [Senators].*
    Alcib. Now the gods keep you old enough, that you
    may live
Only in bone, that none may look on you!
I'm worse than mad: I have kept back their foes,   108
While they have told their money and let out
Their coin upon large interest, I myself
Rich only in large hurts.   All those for this?
Is this the balsam that the usuring senate   112
Pours into captains' wounds?   Banishment!
It comes not ill; I hate not to be banish'd;
It is a cause worthy my spleen and fury,
That I may strike at Athens.   I'll cheer up   116

104 Attend: *await*   spirit: *anger*
107 Only in bone . . . you; *cf. n.*   109 told: *counted*

My discontented troops, and lay for hearts.
'Tis honour with most lands to be at odds;
Soldiers should brook as little wrongs as gods.

Exit.

Scene Six

[*The Same. A Banqueting-room in Timon's House.*

Music. Tables set out.] *Enter divers Friends at
several doors.*

First Lord. The good time of day to you, sir.

Sec. Lord. I also wish it you.   I think this
honourable lord did but try us this other day.   3

First Lord. Upon that were my thoughts
tiring when we encountered: I hope it is not so
low with him as he made it seem in the trial of
his several friends.

Sec. Lord. It should not be, by the persua-
sion of his new feasting.   9

First Lord. I should think so: he hath sent
me an earnest inviting, which many my near
occasions did urge me to put off; but he hath
conjured me beyond them, and I must needs
appear.   14

Sec. Lord. In like manner was I in debt to
my importunate business, but he would not hear
my excuse.   I am sorry, when he sent to borrow
of me, that my provision was out.

First Lord. I am sick of that grief too, as I
understand how all things go.   20

Sec. Lord. Every man here's so.   What would
he have borrowed of you?

First Lord. A thousand pieces.

117 lay for hearts; *cf. n.*   5 tiring: *busily engaged; cf. n.*
11 many: *many of*   near: *important*

Sec. Lord. A thousand pieces!   24
First Lord. What of you?
Third Lord. He sent to me, sir,—Here he comes.

Enter Timon and Attendants.

Tim. With all my heart, gentlemen both: and how fare you?   29

First Lord. Ever at the best, hearing well of your lordship.

Sec. Lord. The swallow follows not summer more willing than we your lordship.   33

Tim. [*Aside.*] Nor more willingly leaves winter; such summer-birds are men.—Gentlemen, our dinner will not recompense this long stay: feast your ears with the music awhile, if they will fare so harshly o' the trumpet's sound; we shall to 't presently.   39

First Lord. I hope it remains not unkindly with your lordship that I returned you an empty messenger.

Tim. O, sir, let it not trouble you.

Sec. Lord. My noble lord,—   44

Tim. Ah, my good friend, what cheer?

Sec. Lord. My most honourable lord, I am e'en sick of shame, that, when your lordship this other day sent to me, I was so unfortunate a beggar.

Tim. Think not on 't, sir.   49

Sec. Lord. If you had sent but two hours before—

Tim. Let it not cumber your better remembrance.   *The banquet brought in.*
Come, bring in all together.

33 willing: *willingly*   38, 39 if they will fare . . . sound; *cf. n.*
52 better remembrance: *remembrance of better things*

Sec. Lord. All covered dishes!

First Lord. Royal cheer, I warrant you.   56

Third Lord. Doubt not that, if money and
the season can yield it.

First Lord. How do you? What's the news?

Third Lord. Alcibiades is banished: hear you
of it?   61

First Lord. } Alcibiades banished!
Sec. Lord. }

Third Lord. 'Tis so, be sure of it.

First Lord. How? how?   64

Sec. Lord. I pray you, upon what?

Tim. My worthy friends, will you draw near?

Third Lord. I'll tell you more anon. Here's
a noble feast toward.   68

Sec. Lord. This is the old man still.

Third Lord. Will 't hold? will 't hold?

Sec. Lord. It does: but time will—and so—

Third Lord. I do conceive.   72

Tim. Each man to his stool, with that spur
as he would to the lip of his mistress: your diet
shall be in all places alike. Make not a city
feast of it, to let the meat cool ere we can agree
upon the first place: sit, sit. The gods require
our thanks.—   78

You great benefactors sprinkle our society
with thankfulness. For your own gifts, make
yourselves praised: but reserve still to give, lest
your deities be despised. Lend to each man
enough, that one need not lend to another, for,
were your godheads to borrow of men, men
would forsake the gods. Make the meat be
beloved more than the man that gives it. Let

68 toward: *at hand*   73 spur: *incentive, eagerness*
75 a city feast: *a formal dinner of municipal functionaries*

no assembly of twenty be without a score of
villains: if there sit twelve women at the table, 88
let a dozen of them—be as they are. The rest of
your fees, O gods,—the senators of Athens, together with the common lag of people,—what is
amiss in them, you gods, make suitable for
destruction. For these my present friends, as
they are to me nothing, so in nothing bless
them, and to nothing are they welcome.
Uncover, dogs, and lap.   96

    [*The dishes are uncovered and are seen to be full
                                of warm water.*]

Some speak. What does his lordship mean?
Some other. I know not.
Tim. May you a better feast never behold,
You knot of mouth-friends! smoke and lukewarm
        water   100
Is your perfection. This is Timon's last;
Who, stuck and spangled with your flatteries,
Washes it off, and sprinkles in your faces

            [*Throwing the water in their faces.*]

Your reeking villainy. Live loath'd, and long, 104
Most smiling, smooth, detested parasites,
Courteous destroyers, affable wolves, meek bears,
You fools of fortune, trencher-friends, time's flies,
Cap-and-knee slaves, vapours, and minute-jacks! 108
Of man and beast the infinite malady
Crust you quite o'er! What, dost thou go?
Soft! take thy physic first—thou too—and thou:—
Stay, I will lend thee money, borrow none.   112

    [*Throws the dishes at them, and drives them out.*]

90 fees: *property* (?)   91 common lag: *lowest class*
100 knot: *band*   smoke: *steam*   101 perfection: *highest excellence*
107 time's flies: *flies of a season; cf. II. ii. 182*
108 minute-jacks; *cf. n.*   109 infinite: *numberless* (?)
111 Soft: *Stay*

What, all in motion?   Henceforth be no feast,
Whereat a villain's not a welcome guest.
Burn, house! sink, Athens! henceforth hated be
Of Timon man and all humanity!   *Exit.*

    Enter the Senators, with other Lords.

    First Lord. How now, my lords!   117
    Sec. Lord. Know you the quality of Lord
Timon's fury?
    Third Lord. Push! did you see my cap?   120
    Fourth Lord. I have lost my gown.
    First Lord. He's but a mad lord, and nought
but humour sways him.   He gave me a jewel th'
other day, and now he has beat it out of my hat.
Did you see my jewel?   125
    Third Lord. Did you see my cap?
    Sec. Lord. Here 'tis.
    Fourth Lord. Here lies my gown.   128
    First Lord. Let's make no stay.
    Sec. Lord. Lord Timon's mad.
    Third Lord.   I feel 't upon my bones.
    Fourth Lord. One day he gives us diamonds, next
day stones.   *Exeunt the Senators [and others].*

ACT FOURTH

Scene One

[Without the Walls of Athens.]

    Enter Timon.

    Tim. Let me look back upon thee.   O thou wall,
That girdlest in those wolves, dive in the earth,

116 Of: *by*   120 Push: *Pshaw*
123 humour: *caprice*   131 stones; *cf. n.*

And fence not Athens! Matrons, turn incontinent!
Obedience fail in children! Slaves and fools,   4
Pluck the grave wrinkled senate from the bench,
And minister in their steads! To general filths
Convert, o' the instant, green virginity!
Do 't in your parents' eyes! Bankrupts, hold fast;   8
Rather than render back, out with your knives,
And cut your trusters' throats! Bound servants, steal!
Large-handed robbers your grave masters are,
And pill by law. Maid, to thy master's bed;   12
Thy mistress is o' the brothel! Son of sixteen,
Pluck the lin'd crutch from thy old limping sire:
With it beat out his brains! Piety and fear,
Religion to the gods, peace, justice, truth,   16
Domestic awe, night-rest and neighbourhood
Instruction, manners, mysteries and trades,
Degrees, observances, customs and laws,
Decline to your confounding contraries,   20
And let confusion live! Plagues incident to men,
Your potent and infectious fevers heap
On Athens, ripe for stroke! Thou cold sciatica,
Cripple our senators, that their limbs may halt   24
As lamely as their manners! Lust and liberty
Creep in the minds and marrows of our youth,
That 'gainst the stream of virtue they may strive,
And drown themselves in riot! Itches, blains,   28
Sow all the Athenian bosoms, and their crop
Be general leprosy! Breath infect breath,
That their society, as their friendship, may
Be merely poison! Nothing I'll bear from thee   32
But nakedness, thou detestable town!

6 filths: *strumpets*   7 Convert: *turn*
9 render back: *repay*   12 pill: *plunder*   14 lin'd: *stuffed*
17 Domestic awe: *respect for parents*   neighbourhood: *neighborly*
   feeling   18 mysteries: *crafts*   20 confounding: *ruinous*
25 liberty: *license*   28 blains: *sores*   32 merely: *entirely*

Take thou that too, with multiplying bans!
Timon will to the woods, where he shall find
The unkindest beast more kinder than mankind.   36
The gods confound—hear me, you good gods all!—
The Athenians both within and out that wall!
And grant, as Timon grows, his hate may grow
To the whole race of mankind, high and low!   40
                                        Amen.   *Exit.*

Scene Two

[*Athens.   Timon's House*]

Enter Steward [Flavius], with two or three servants.

  First Serv. Hear you, master steward, where's our
    master?
Are we undone? cast off? nothing remaining?
  Flav. Alack, my fellows, what should I say to you?
Let me be recorded by the righteous gods,   4
I am as poor as you.
  First Serv.   Such a house broke!
So noble a master fall'n! All gone! and not
One friend to take his fortune by the arm,
And go along with him!
  Sec. Serv.   As we do turn our backs   8
From our companion thrown into his grave,
So his familiars to his buried fortunes
Slink all away; leave their false vows with him,
Like empty purses pick'd; and his poor self,   12
A dedicated beggar to the air,
With his disease of all-shunn'd poverty,
Walks, like contempt, alone. More of our fellows.

34 multiplying: *increasing*   bans: *curses*   38 out: *without*
4 recorded: *taken to witness*
10 familiars . . . fortunes: *those who were so intimate with his now*
    buried prosperity
13 *A beggar devoted by fortune to a homeless life*

Enter other Servants.

Flav. All broken implements of a ruin'd house.   16
  Third Serv. Yet do our hearts wear Timon's
    livery;
That see I by our faces; we are fellows still,
Serving alike in sorrow: leak'd is our bark,
And we, poor mates, stand on the dying deck,   20
Hearing the surges threat: we must all part
Into this sea of air.
  Flav.   Good fellows all,
The latest of my wealth I'll share amongst you.
Wherever we shall meet, for Timon's sake   24
Let's yet be fellows; let's shake our heads, and say,
As 'twere a knell unto our master's fortunes,
'We have seen better days.' Let each take some.
Nay, put out all your hands. Not one word more: 28
Thus part we rich in sorrow, parting poor.
        [They] embrace and part several ways.
O, the fierce wretchedness that glory brings us.
Who would not wish to be from wealth exempt,
Since riches point to misery and contempt?   32
Who would be so mock'd with glory? or to live
But in a dream of friendship?
To have his pomp and all what state compounds
But only painted, like his varnish'd friends?   36
Poor honest lord, brought low by his own heart,
Undone by goodness. Strange, unusual blood,
When man's worst sin is he does too much good!
Who then dares to be half so kind again?   40
For bounty, that makes gods, does still mar men.
My dearest lord, blest, to be most accurs'd,
Rich only to be wretched, thy great fortunes

18 fellows: *comrades*   29 S. d. several ways: *in different directions*
33 to live: *desire to live*   35 all . . . compounds; *cf. n.*
38 blood: *temper*

Are made thy chief afflictions. Alas, kind lord!   44
He's flung in rage from this ingrateful seat
Of monstrous friends;
Nor has he with him to supply his life,
Or that which can command it.   48
I'll follow and inquire him out:
I'll ever serve his mind with my best will;
Whilst I have gold I'll be his steward still.   *Exit.*

Scene Three

[*Woods and Cave near the Sea-shore*]

Enter Timon in the Woods [*from the Cave*]

Tim. O blessed breeding sun, draw from the earth
Rotten humidity; below thy sister's orb
Infect the air! Twinn'd brothers of one womb,
Whose procreation, residence and birth,   4
Scarce is dividant, touch them with several fortunes,
The greater scorns the lesser: not nature,
To whom all sores lay siege, can bear great fortune
But by contempt of nature.   8
Raise me this beggar, and deny 't that lord,
The senator shall bear contempt hereditary,
The beggar native honour.
It is the pasture lards the rother's sides,   12
The want that makes him lean. Who dares, who
    dares,
In purity of manhood stand upright,
And say, 'This man's a flatterer'?   If one be,
So are they all; for every grize of fortune   16

46 monstrous: *unnatural*
47 to supply his life: *the necessities of life*
5 dividant: *divided*   9 Raise me . . . lord; *cf. n.*
12 rother's: *ox's; cf. n.*   16 grize: *step*

Is smooth'd by that below: the learned pate
Ducks to the golden fool: all is oblique;
There's nothing level in our cursed natures
But direct villainy. Therefore, be abhorr'd   20
All feasts, societies, and throngs of men!
His semblable, yea, himself, Timon disdains:
Destruction fang mankind! Earth, yield me roots!
                                                      [*Digging.*]
Who seeks for better of thee, sauce his palate   24
With thy most operant poison! What is here?
Gold? yellow, glittering, precious gold? No, goas,
I am no idle votarist: roots, you clear heavens!
Thus much of this will make black white, foul
    fair,   28
Wrong right, base noble, old young, coward valiant.
Ha, you gods! why this? what this, you gods? Why,
    this
Will lug your priests and servants from your sides,
Pluck stout men's pillows from below their heads: 32
This yellow slave
Will knit and break religions; bless the accurs'd;
Make the hoar leprosy ador'd; place thieves,
And give them title, knee, and approbation,   36
With senators on the bench: this is it
That makes the wappen'd widow wed again;
She, whom the spital-house and ulcerous sores
Would cast the gorge at, this embalms and spices   40
To the April day again. Come, damned earth,
Thou common whore of mankind, that putt'st odds
Among the rout of nations, I will make thee

17 smooth'd: *flattered*   18 oblique: *indirect*
22 semblable: *counterpart*   23 fang: *seize*
25 operant: *potent*   27 idle: *empty*   votarist: *votary; cf. n.*
32 Pluck . . . heads; *cf. n.*   stout: *strong*
38 wappen'd: *stale* (?)
39, 40 spital-house . . . cast the gorge at: *hospital patients or victims
    of ulcerous sores would loathe*

Do thy right nature. *March afar off.* Ha! a drum?
    thou'rt quick,   44
But yet I'll bury thee: thou'lt go, strong thief,
When gouty keepers of thee cannot stand:
Nay, stay thou out for earnest. [*Keeping some gold.*]

Enter Alcibiades, with drum and fife, in warlike
manner; and Phrynia and Timandra.

   Alcib. What art thou there? speak.   48
   Tim. A beast, as thou art. The canker gnaw thy
    heart,
For showing me again the eyes of man!
   Alcib. What is thy name? Is man so hateful to
    thee,
That art thyself a man?   52
   Tim. I am 'Misanthropos,' and hate mankind.
For thy part, I do wish thou wert a dog,
That I might love thee something.
   Alcib.   I know thee well,
But in thy fortunes am unlearn'd and strange.   56
   Tim. I know thee too; and more than that I know
    thee
I not desire to know. Follow thy drum;
With man's blood paint the ground, gules, gules:
Religious canons, civil laws are cruel;   60
Then what should war be? This fell whore of thine
Hath in her more destruction than thy sword
For all her cherubin look.
   Phry.   Thy lips rot off!
   Tim. I will not kiss thee; then the rot returns   64
To thine own lips again.

44 Do . . . nature; *cf. n.*   quick: *living (a pun)*
47 earnest: *money paid as an instalment to secure a bargain*
53 'Misanthropos': *Hater of Mankind; cf. n.*
55 something: *somewhat*   56 strange: *unacquainted*
59 gules: *the heraldic term for red*   61 fell: *deadly*

Alcib. How came the noble Timon to this change?

Tim. As the moon does, by wanting light to give:
But then renew I could not like the moon;   68
There were no suns to borrow of.

Alcib. Noble Timon, what friendship may I do
    thee?

Tim. None, but to maintain my opinion.

    Alcib. What is it, Timon?   72

    Tim. Promise me friendship, but perform
none: if thou wilt not promise, the gods plague
thee, for thou art a man: if thou dost perform,
confound thee, for thou art a man!   76

Alcib. I have heard in some sort of thy miseries.

Tim. Thou saw'st them, when I had prosperity.

Alcib. I see them now; then was a blessed time.

Tim. As thine is now, held with a brace of har-
    lots.   80

Timan. Is this the Athenian minion, whom the
    world
Voic'd so regardfully?

    Tim.   Art thou Timandra?

    Timan.   Yes.

Tim. Be a whore still; they love thee not that use
    thee;
Give them diseases, leaving with thee their lust.   84
Make use of thy salt hours: season the slaves
For tubs and baths; bring down rose-cheeked youth
To the tub-fast and the diet.

    Timan.   Hang thee, monster!

Alcib. Pardon him, sweet Timandra, for his
    wits   88
Are drown'd and lost in his calamities.

---

77 in some sort: *in a way*   81 minion: *darling*
82 Voic'd: *acclaimed*   regardfully: *respectfully*
85 salt: *wanton*   87 To the tub-fast and the diet; *cf. n.*

I have but little gold of late, brave Timon,
The want whereof doth daily make revolt
In my penurious band: I have heard and griev'd   92
How cursed Athens, mindless of thy worth,
Forgetting thy great deeds, when neighbour states,
But for thy sword and fortune, trod upon them—
    Tim. I prithee, beat thy drum, and get thee
        gone.   96
    Alcib. I am thy friend and pity thee, dear Timon.
    Tim: How dost thou pity him whom thou dost
        trouble?
I had rather be alone.
    Alcib.   Why, fare thee well:
Here is some gold for thee.
    Tim.   Keep it, I cannot eat it.   100
    Alcib. When I have laid proud Athens on a heap—
    Tim. Warr'st thou 'gainst Athens?
    Alcib. Ay, Timon, and have cause.
    Tim. The gods confound them all in thy conquest,
        and   104
Thee after, when thou hast conquer'd!
    Alcib.   Why me, Timon?
    Tim. That by killing of villains thou wast born to
        conquer
My country.
Put up thy gold: go on,—here's gold,—go on;   108
Be as a planetary plague, when Jove
Will o'er some high-vic'd city hang his poison
In the sick air: let not thy sword skip one
Pity not honour'd age for his white beard;   112
He is a usurer.   Strike me the counterfeit matron;
It is her habit only that is honest,

92 penurious: *poverty-stricken*   94 neighbour: *neighboring*
101 on: *in*   109 planetary plague; *cf. n.*
113 counterfeit: *deceitful*   114 habit: *demeanor*

Herself's a bawd. Let not the virgin's cheek
Make soft thy trenchant sword; for those milk-
          paps,   116
That through the window-bars bore at men's eyes,
Are not within the leaf of pity writ,
But set them down horrible traitors. Spare not the
     babe,
Whose dimpled smiles from fools exhaust their
          mercy;   120
Think it a bastard whom the oracle
Hath doubtfully pronounc'd thy throat shall cut,
And mince it sans remorse. Swear against objects;
Put armour on thine ears and on thine eyes,   124
Whose proof nor yells of mothers, maids, nor babes,
Nor sight of priests in holy vestments bleeding,
Shall pierce a jot. There's gold to pay thy soldiers:
Make large confusion; and, thy fury spent,   128
Confounded be thyself! Speak not, be gone.

     Alcib. Hast thou gold yet? I'll take the gold thou
          giv'st me,
Not all thy counsel.

     Tim. Dost thou or dost thou not, heaven's curse
          upon thee!   132

     Phr.   ⎱ Give us some gold, good Timon: hast thou
     Timan. ⎰   more?

     Tim. Enough to make a whore forswear her trade,
And to make whores, a bawd. Hold up, you sluts,
Your aprons mountant: you are not oathable;   136
Although, I know, you'll swear, terribly swear

117 window-bars: *latticed open-work of the bodice*   bore at: *show*
        themselves to   121 whom: *who*
122 doubtfully: *ambiguously*
123 sans: *without*   objects: *objects of commiseration*
125 proof: *impenetrability*   128 confusion: *destruction*
132 Dost . . . not: *whether you do or not*
134, 135 Enough . . . bawd; *cf. n.*
136 mountant: *rising*   oathable: *fit to swear a true oath*

Into strong shudders and to heavenly agues
The immortal gods that hear you; spare your oaths,
I'll trust to your conditions: be whores still;　　140
And he whose pious breath seeks to convert you,
Be strong in whore, allure him, burn him up;
Let your close fire predominate his smoke,
And be no turncoats: yet may your pains, six
　　　months,　　144
Be quite contrary: and thatch your poor thin roofs
With burdens of the dead;—some that were hang'd,
No matter:—wear them, betray with them: whore
　　　still;
Paint till a horse may mire upon your face:　　148
A pox of wrinkles!

　　Phr. ⎱ Well, more gold. What then?
　　Timan. ⎰

Believe 't, that we'll do anything for gold.

　　Tim. Consumptions sow　　152
In hollow bones of man; strike their sharp shins,
And mar men's spurring. Crack the lawyer's voice,
That he may never more false title plead,
Nor sound his quillets shrilly: hoar the flamen,　　156
That scolds against the quality of flesh
And not believes himself: down with the nose,
Down with it flat; take the bridge quite away
Of him that, his particular to foresee,　　160
Smells from the general weal: make curl'd-pate ruf-
　　　fians bald;
And let the unscarr'd braggarts of the war
Derive some pain from you: plague all,
That your activity may defeat and quell　　164

140 conditions: *characters*　　145, 146 and thatch . . . dead; *cf. n.*
156 quillets: *verbal niceties*　　hoar: *make mouldy*　　flamen: *priest*
160 particular: *personal interest*
161 Smells from: *loses the scent of*

The source of all erection.   There's more gold:
Do you damn others, and let this damn you,
And ditches grave you all!

    Phr.   ⎱ More counsel with more money, bounteous
    Timan.⎰   Timon.   168

    Tim. More whore, more mischief first; I have given
        you earnest.

    Alcib. Strike up the drum towards Athens! Fare-
        well, Timon:
If I thrive well, I'll visit thee again.

    Tim. If I hope well, I'll never see thee more.   172
    Alcib. I never did thee harm.
    Tim. Yes, thou spok'st well of me.
    Alcib.   Call'st thou that harm?
    Tim. Men daily find it. Get thee away, and take
Thy beagles with thee.
    Alcib.   We but offend him. Strike!   176

        [*Drum beats.*]   *Exeunt* [*Alcibiades, Phrynia,*
                            and Timandra].

    Tim. That nature, being sick of man's unkind-
        ness,
Should yet be hungry! Common mother, thou,
                           [*Digging.*]
Whose womb unmeasurable, and infinite breast,
Teems, and feeds all; whose self-same mettle,   180
Whereof thy proud child, arrogant man, is puff'd,
Engenders the black toad and adder blue,
The gilded newt and eyeless venom'd worm,
With all the abhorred births below crisp heaven   184
Whereon Hyperion's quickening fire doth shine;
Yield him, who all thy human sons doth hate,

167 grave: *bury*   172 hope well: *attain my hope*
176 beagles: *small variety of hound, used contemptuously of women*
184 crisp: *wavy, with clouds*   185 Hyperion; *cf. n.*

From forth thy plenteous bosom, one poor root!
Ensear thy fertile and conceptious womb,   188
Let it no more bring out ingrateful man!
Go great with tigers, dragons, wolves, and bears;
Teem with new monsters, whom thy upward face
Hath to the marbled mansion all above   192
Never presented!—O, a root! dear thanks!—
Dry up thy marrows, vines, and plough-torn leas;
Whereof ingrateful man, with liquorish draughts
And morsels unctuous, greases his pure mind,   196
That from it all consideration slips!

Enter Apemantus.

More man? Plague, plague!
    Apem. I was directed hither: men report
Thou dost affect my manners, and dost use them.   200
    Tim. 'Tis then because thou dost not keep a dog,
Whom I would imitate: consumption catch thee!
    Apem. This is in thee a nature but infected;
A poor unmanly melancholy sprung   204
From change of fortune. Why this spade? this place?
This slave-like habit? and these looks of care?
Thy flatterers yet wear silk, drink wine, lie soft,
Hug their diseas'd perfumes, and have forgot   208
That ever Timon was. Shame not these woods
By putting on the cunning of a carper.
Be thou a flatterer now, and seek to thrive
By that which has undone thee: hinge thy knee,   212
And let his very breath whom thou'lt observe
Blow off thy cap; praise his most vicious strain,

188 conceptious: *fruitful*   192 marbled: *shining like marble*
195 liquorish: *pleasant*   196 unctuous: *oily*
197 consideration: *regard for higher things*
203 infected: *affected*   208 perfumes: *perfumed mistresses*
210 cunning: *profession*   carper: *censurer*   212 hinge: *bend*
213 observe: *pay court to*   214 strain: *quality*

And call it excellent. Thou wast told thus;
Thou gav'st thine ears, like tapsters that bade wel-
    come,   216
To knaves and all approachers: 'tis most just
That thou turn rascal; hadst thou wealth again,
Rascals should have 't. Do not assume my likeness.
   Tim. Were I like thee I'd throw away myself.   220
   Apem. Thou hast cast away thyself, being like thy-
    self,
A madman so long, now a fool. What, think'st
That the bleak air, thy boisterous chamberlain,
Will put thy shirt on warm? will these moss'd
    trees,   224
That have outliv'd the eagle, page thy heels
And skip when thou point'st out? will the cold brook,
Candied with ice, caudle thy morning taste,
To cure the o'er-night's surfeit? Call the crea-
    tures   228
Whose naked natures live in all the spite
Of wreakful heaven, whose bare unhoused trunks
To the conflicting elements expos'd,
Answer mere nature; bid them flatter thee;   232
O, thou shalt find—
   Tim.   A fool of thee. Depart.
   Apem. I love thee better now than e'er I did.
   Tim. I hate thee worse.
   Apem.   Why?
   Tim.   Thou flatter'st misery.
   Apem. I flatter not, but say thou art a caitiff.   236
   Tim. Why dost thou seek me out?
   Apem.   To vex thee.

---

224 warm: *heated moderately*   225 page: *follow like a page*
227 Candied: *crystallized with frost*   caudle: *serve as a warm drink*
230 wreakful: *revengeful*   232 Answer mere nature; *cf. n.*

   Tim. Always a villain's office, or a fool's.
Dost please thyself in 't?
   Apem.   Ay.
   Tim.   What! a knave too?
   Apem. If thou didst put this sour-cold habit
on   240
To castigate thy pride, 'twere well: but thou
Dost it enforcedly; thou'dst courtier be again,
Wert thou not beggar. Willing misery
Outlives incertain pomp, is crown'd before: 244
The one is filling still, never complete;
The other, at high wish: best state, contentless,
Hath a distracted and most wretched being,
Worse than the worst, content.   248
Thou shouldst desire to die, being miserable.
   Tim. Not by his breath that is more miserable.
Thou art a slave, whom Fortune's tender arm
With favour never clasp'd, but bred a dog.   252
Hadst thou, like us from our first swath, proceeded
The sweet degrees that this brief world affords
To such as may the passive drudges of it
Freely command, thou wouldst have plung'd thy-
self   256
In general riot, melted down thy youth
In different beds of lust, and never learn'd
The icy precepts of respect, but follow'd
The sugar'd game before thee. But myself,   260
Who had the world as my confectionary,
The mouths, the tongues, the eyes, and hearts of men
At duty, more than I could frame employment,

238, 239 Always . . . too; *cf. n.*
248 *Far worse than the worst condition of life when accompanied by*
    content   250 breath: *voice, advice*
253 swath: *swaddling-clothes*
253, 254 proceeded . . . degrees; *cf. n.*   255 drudges; *cf. n.*
261 confectionary: *maker of sweet-meats*   263 frame: *provide with*

That numberless upon me stuck as leaves　　　　264
Do on the oak, have with one winter's brush
Fell from their boughs, and left me open, bare
For every storm that blows: I, to bear this,
That never knew but better, is some burden:　　268
Thy nature did commence in sufferance, time
Hath made thee hard in 't.　Why shouldst thou hate
　　men?
They never flatter'd thee: what hast thou given?
If thou wilt curse, thy father, that poor rag,　　272
Must be thy subject, who in spite put stuff
To some she beggar and compounded thee
Poor rogue hereditary.　Hence, be gone!
If thou hadst not been born the worst of men,　276
Thou hadst been a knave and flatterer.
　　Apem.　　　　　　　　Art thou proud yet?
　　Tim. Ay, that I am not thee.
　　Apem.　　　　　　　　I, that I was
No prodigal.
　　Tim.　　　I, that I am one now:
Were all the wealth I have shut up in thee,　　280
I'd give thee leave to hang it.　Get thee gone.
That the whole life of Athens were in this!
Thus would I eat it.　　　　　　[*Eating a root.*]
　　Apem.　　　　　Here; I will mend thy feast.
　　　　　　　　　　　　　[*Offering him a root.*]
　　Tim. First mend my company; take away thy-
　　　self.　　　　　　　　　　　　284
　　Apem. So I shall mend mine own, by the lack of
　　　thine.

265 have: *i.e., and now have*　　brush: *violence*
269 sufferance: *suffering*　　　　270 hard in: *hardened to*
272 rag: *term of contempt, a shabby person*
275 hereditary: *by heredity*　　　　282 That: *would that*

Tim. 'Tis not well mended so, it is but botch'd;
If not, I would it were.

Apem. What wouldst thou have to Athens?   288

Tim. Thee thither in a whirlwind. If thou wilt,
Tell them there I have gold; look, so I have.

Apem. Here is no use for gold.

Tim.   The best and truest;
For here it sleeps, and does no hired harm.   292

Apem. Where liest o' nights, Timon?

Tim.   Under that's above me.
Where feed'st thou o' days, Apemantus?

Apem. Where my stomach finds meat; or,
rather, where I eat it.   296

Tim. Would poison were obedient and knew my
mind!

Apem. Where wouldst thou send it?

Tim. To sauce thy dishes.   299

Apem. The middle of humanity thou never
knewest, but the extremity of both ends: when
thou wast in thy gilt and thy perfume, they
mocked thee for too much curiosity; in thy
rags thou know'st none, but art despised for
the contrary. There's a medlar for thee; eat it.

Tim. On what I hate I feed not.   306

Apem. Dost hate a medlar?

Tim. Ay, though it look like thee.

Apem. An thou hadst hated meddlers sooner,
thou shouldst have loved thyself better now.
What man didst thou ever know unthrift that
was beloved after his means?   312

Tim. Who, without those means thou talk'st
of, didst thou ever know beloved?

286, 287 'Tis not . . . would it were; *cf. n.*
288 What . . . Athens; *cf. n.*   303 curiosity: *fastidiousness*
305 medlar; *cf. n.*   311 unthrift: *prodigal*   312 after; *cf. n.*

Apem. Myself.

Tim. I understand thee; thou hadst some
means to keep a dog.   317

Apem. What things in the world canst thou
nearest compare to thy flatterers?

Tim. Women nearest; but men, men are the
things themselves. What wouldst thou do with
the world, Apemantus, if it lay in thy power?

Apem. Give it the beasts, to be rid of the
men.   324

Tim. Wouldst thou have thyself fall in the
confusion of men, and remain a beast with the
beasts?

Apem. Ay, Timon.   328

Tim. A beastly ambition, which the gods
grant thee t' attain to! If thou wert the lion,
the fox would beguile thee: if thou wert the
lamb, the fox would eat thee: if thou wert the
fox, the lion would suspect thee, when perad-
venture thou wert accused by the ass: if thou
wert the ass, thy dulness would torment thee,
and still thou livedst but as a breakfast to the
wolf: if thou wert the wolf, thy greediness
would afflict thee, and oft thou shouldst hazard
thy life for thy dinner: wert thou the unicorn,
pride and wrath would confound thee, and make 340
thine own self the conquest of thy fury: wert
thou a bear, thou wouldst be killed by the
horse: wert thou a horse, thou wouldst be
seized by the leopard: wert thou a leopard,
thou wert german to the lion, and the spots of
thy kindred were jurors on thy life: all thy

326 confusion: *ruin*   339 wert thou the unicorn, etc.; *cf. n.*
340 confound: *destroy*   344-346 wert thou . . . life; *cf. n.*
345 german: *akin*

safety were remotion, and thy defence absence.
What beast couldst thou be, that were not
subject to a beast? and what a beast art thou
already, that seest not thy loss in transforma-
tion!   351

Apem. If thou couldst please me with speaking to me, thou mightst have hit upon it here:
the commonwealth of Athens is become a forest
of beasts.

Tim. How has the ass broke the wall, that
thou art out of the city?   357

Apem. Yonder comes a poet and a painter:
the plague of company light upon thee! I will
fear to catch it, and give way. When I know
not what else to do, I'll see thee again.   361

Tim. When there is nothing living but thee,
thou shalt be welcome. I had rather be a beg-
gar's dog than Apemantus.   364

Apem. Thou art the cap of all the fools alive.
Tim. Would thou wert clean enough to spit upon!
Apem. A plague on thee! thou art too bad to curse.
Tim. All villains that do stand by thee are
pure.   368
Apem. There is no leprosy but what thou speak'st.
Tim. If I name thee,
I'll beat thee; but I should infect my hands.
Apem. I would my tongue could rot them off!   372
Tim. Away, thou issue of a mangy dog!
Choler does kill me that thou art alive;
I swound to see thee.
Apem.   Would thou wouldst burst!
Tim.   Away,
Thou tedious rogue! I am sorry I shall lose   376

347 remotion: *keeping away*   358 Yonder . . . painter; *cf. n.*
365 cap: *chief*   375 swound: *swoon*

A stone by thee.   [*Throws a stone at him.*]
   Apem.   Beast!
   Tim.   Slave!
   Apem.   Toad!
   Tim.   Rogue, rogue, rogue!
I am sick of this false world, and will love nought
But even the mere necessities upon 't.
Then, Timon, presently prepare thy grave;   380
Lie where the light foam of the sea may beat
Thy grave-stone daily: make thine epitaph,
That death in me at others' lives may laugh.
                         [*Looking on the gold.*]
O thou sweet king-killer, and dear divorce   384
'Twixt natural son and sire! thou bright defiler
Of Hymen's purest bed! thou valiant Mars!
Thou ever young, fresh, lov'd, and delicate wooer,
Whose blush doth thaw the consecrated snow
That lies on Dian's lap! thou visible god,   389
That solder'st close impossibilities,
And mak'st them kiss! that speak'st with every
        tongue,
To every purpose! O thou touch of hearts!   392
Think thy slave, man, rebels; and by thy virtue
Set them into confounding odds, that beasts
May have the world in empire!
   Apem.   Would 'twere so!
But not till I am dead. I'll say thou'st gold: 396
Thou wilt be throng'd to shortly.
   Tim.   Throng'd to!
   Apem.   Ay.
   Tim. Thy back, I prithee.
   Apem.   Live, and love thy misery!

380 presently. *immediately*   384 dear: *used intensively*
386 Hymen, *cf. n.*   390 close: *closely* (?)
392 touch: *touchstone*

Tim. Long live so, and so die!   *Exit Apemantus.*
                              I am quit.
Moe things like men?   Eat, Timon, and abhor
them.   400
                    Enter the Banditti.

First Ban. Where should he have this gold?
It is some poor fragment, some slender ort of
his remainder; the mere want of gold, and the
falling-from of his friends, drove him into this
melancholy.   405
Sec. Ban. It is noised he hath a mass of
treasure.
Third Ban. Let us make the assay upon
him: if he care not for 't, he will supply us
easily; if he covetously reserve it, how shall's
get it?
Sec. Ban. True; for he bears it not about him; 'tis
hid.   412
First Ban. Is not this he?
All. Where?
Sec. Ban. 'Tis his description.
Third Ban. He; I know him.   416
All. Save thee, Timon.
Tim. Now, thieves?
All. Soldiers, not thieves.
Tim. Both too; and women's sons.   420
All. We are not thieves, but men that much do want.
Tim. Your greatest want is, you want much of
meat.
Why should you want?   Behold, the earth hath roots;
Within this mile break forth a hundred springs;   424

399 quit: *rid of you*   402 ort: *fragment*
404 falling-from: *desertion*   407 assay: *trial*
410 shall's: *shall we*   418 Now: *how now*

The oaks bear mast, the briers scarlet hips;
The bounteous housewife, nature, on each bush
Lays her full mess before you. Want! why want?
   First Ban. We cannot live on grass, on berries,
     water,   428
As beasts and birds and fishes.
   Tim. Nor on the beasts themselves, the birds, and
     fishes;
You must eat men. Yet thanks I must you con
That you are thieves profess'd, that you work not 432
In holier shapes: for there is boundless theft
In limited professions. Rascal thieves,
Here's gold. Go, suck the subtle blood o' the grape,
Till the high fever seethe your blood to froth,   436
And so 'scape hanging: trust not the physician;
His antidotes are poison, and he slays
Moe than you rob: take wealth and lives together;
Do villainy, do, since you protest to do 't,   440
Like workmen. I'll example you with thievery:
The sun's a thief, and with his great attraction
Robs the vast sea: the moon's an arrant thief,
And her pale fire she snatches from the sun: 444
The sea's a thief, whose liquid surge resolves
The moon into salt tears: the earth's a thief,
That feeds and breeds by a composture stol'n
From general excrement: each thing's a thief: 448
The laws, your curb and whip, in their rough power
Have uncheck'd theft. Love not yourselves; away!
Rob one another. There's more gold. Cut throats:
All that you meet are thieves: to Athens go,   452
Break open shops; nothing can you steal,

---

425 mast: *fruit of the beech, oak, or chestnut*   hips: *fruit of the wild*
   rose   427 mess: *dish (of food)*
431 thanks . . . con: *be grateful*   434 limited: *restricted*
440 protest: *vow*   441 example: *furnish with instances*
445, 446 whose liquid . . . tears; *cf. n.*   447 composture: *manure*

But thieves do lose it: steal not less for this
I give you; and gold confound you howsoe'er!
Amen.   456

    Third Ban. Has almost charmed me from
my profession by persuading me to it.

    First Ban. 'Tis in the malice of mankind
that he thus advises us; not to have us thrive in
our mystery.   461

    Sec. Ban. I'll believe him as an enemy, and
give over my trade.

    First Ban. Let us first see peace in Athens:
there is no time so miserable but a man may be
true.   *Exeunt Thieves.*

   Enter the Steward [*Flavius*] *to Timon.*

    Flav. O you gods!
Is yond despised and ruinous man my lord?   468
Full of decay and failing?   O monument
And wonder of good deeds evilly bestow'd!
What an alteration of honour
Has desperate want made!   472
What viler thing upon the earth than friends
Who can bring noblest minds to basest ends!
How rarely does it meet with this time's guise,
When man was wish'd to love his enemies!   476
Grant I may ever love, and rather woo
Those that would mischief me than those that do!
Has caught me in his eye: I will present
My honest grief unto him, and, as my lord,   480
Still serve him with my life.   My dearest master!

    [*Timon comes forward.*]

    Tim. Away! what art thou?

466 true: *honest*   471 alteration of honour: *change to dishonor*
475 rarely: *finely*   475, 476 How rarely . . . enemies; *cf. n.*
477, 478 Grant . . . that do; *cf. n.*

Flav.   Have you forgot me, sir?

Tim. Why dost ask that? I have forgot all men;
Then, if thou grant'st thou'rt a man, I have forgot
    thee.   484

Flav. An honest poor servant of yours.

Tim.   Then I know thee not:
I never had an honest man about me, I; all
I kept were knaves, to serve in meat to villains.

Flav. The gods are witness,   488
Ne'er did poor steward wear a truer grief
For his undone lord than mine eyes for you.

Tim. What, dost thou weep? come nearer; then I
    love thee,
Because thou art a woman, and disclaim'st   492
Flinty mankind, whose eyes do never give,
But thorough lust and laughter. Pity's sleeping:
Strange times, that weep with laughing, not with
    weeping!

Flav. I beg of you to know me, good my lord,   496
To accept my grief and whilst this poor wealth lasts
To entertain me as your steward still.

Tim. Had I a steward
So true, so just, and now so comfortable?   500
It almost turns my dangerous nature mild.
Let me behold thy face. Surely this man
Was born of woman.
Forgive my general and exceptless rashness,   504
You perpetual-sober gods! I do proclaim
One honest man—mistake me not—but one;
No more, I pray,—and he's a steward.
How fain would I have hated all mankind!   508
And thou redeem'st thyself: but all, save thee,

---

493 give: *shed tears*   494 thorough: *through*
498 entertain: *maintain, use*   500 comfortable: *helpful*
504 exceptless: *making no exception*

I fell with curses.
Methinks thou art more honest now than wise;
For, by oppressing and betraying me,   512
Thou mightst have sooner got another service:
For many so arrive at second masters,
Upon their first lord's neck. But tell me true—
For I must ever doubt, though ne'er so sure—   516
Is not thy kindness subtle, covetous,
If not a usuring kindness and as rich men deal gifts,
Expecting in return twenty for one?
    Flav. No, my most worthy master; in whose
        breast   520
Doubt and suspect, alas, are plac'd too late:
You should have fear'd false times when you did
        feast:
Suspect still comes when an estate is least.
That which I show, heaven knows, is merely love,   524
Duty and zeal to your unmatched mind,
Care of your food and living; and, believe it,
My most honour'd lord,
For any benefit that points to me,   528
Either in hope, or present, I'd exchange
For this one wish, that you had power and wealth
To requite me by making rich yourself.
    Tim. Look thee, 'tis so! Thou singly honest
        man,   532
Here, take: the gods out of my misery,
Have sent thee treasure. Go, live rich and happy;
But thus condition'd: thou shalt build from men,
Hate all, curse all, show charity to none,   536
But let the famish'd flesh slide from the bone,
Ere thou relieve the beggar: give to dogs
What thou deny'st to men; let prisons swallow 'em,

521 suspect: *suspicion*   525 unmatched: *matchless*
532 singly: *uniquely*   535 thus condition'd: *on these conditions*

Debts wither 'em to nothing: be men like blasted
    woods,   540
And may diseases lick up their false bloods!
And so, farewell, and thrive.
    Flav.   O, let me stay
And comfort you, my master.
    Tim.   If thou hatest
Curses, stay not: fly, whilst thou'rt blest and free: 544
Ne'er see thou man, and let me ne'er see thee.   *Exit.*

ACT FIFTH

Scene One

[The Woods.   Before Timon's Cave]

Enter Poet and Painter.

    Pain. As I took note of the place, it cannot
be far where he abides.

    Poet. What's to be thought of him? Does
the rumour hold for true that he's so full of
gold?   5

    Pain. Certain: Alcibiades reports it; Phrynia
and Timandra had gold of him: he likewise
enriched poor straggling soldiers with great
quantity: 'tis said he gave unto his steward a
mighty sum.   10

    Poet. Then this breaking of his has been but
a try for his friends.

    Pain. Nothing else: you shall see him a
palm in Athens again, and flourish with the
highest.   Therefore 'tis not amiss we tender our 15

4 hold for: *prove*   12 try: *test*

loves to him in this supposed distress of his: it
will show honestly in us, and is very likely to
load our purposes with what they travail for, if it
be a just and true report that goes of his having.

Poet. What have you now to present unto him? 20

Pain. Nothing at this time but my visitation:
only I will promise him an excellent piece.

Poet. I must serve him so too, tell him of an
intent that's coming towards him.   24

Pain. Good as the best. Promising is the
very air o' the time: it opens the eyes of ex-
pectation: performance is ever the duller for his
act; and, but in the plainer and simpler kind of
people, the deed of saying is quite out of use. 29
To promise is most courtly and fashionable:
performance is a kind of will or testament which
argues a great sickness in his judgement that
makes it.   33

Enter Timon from his Cave.

Tim. [*Aside.*] Excellent workman! Thou
canst not paint a man so bad as is thyself.

Poet. I am thinking what I shall say I have
provided for him: it must be a personating of
himself; a satire against the softness of prosperity, with a discovery of the infinite flatteries
that follow youth and opulency.   40

Tim. [*Aside.*] Must thou needs stand for a
villain in thine own work? Wilt thou whip
thine own faults in other men? Do so, I have
gold for thee.   44

Poet. Nay, let's seek him:
Then do we sin against our own estate,

18 purposes: *plans*   29 deed of saying: *performance of promise*
37 personating: *representing*
                              39 discovery: *showing*

When we may profit meet, and come too late.

    Pain. True;   48

When the day serves, before black-corner'd night,

Find what thou want'st by free and offer'd light.

Come.

    Tim. [*Aside.*] I'll meet you at the turn. What a

        god's gold,   52

That he is worshipp'd in a baser temple

Than where swine feed!

'Tis thou that rigg'st the bark and plough'st the foam,

Settlest admired reverence in a slave: 56

To thee be worship! and thy saints for aye

Be crown'd with plagues, that thee alone obey!

Fit I meet them.   [*Coming forward.*]

    Poet. Hail, worthy Timon!

    Pain.   Our late noble master!   60

    Tim. Have I once liv'd to see two honest men?

    Poet. Sir,

Having often of your open bounty tasted,

Hearing you were retir'd, your friends fall'n off, 64

Whose thankless natures—O abhorred spirits!

Not all the whips of heaven are large enough—

What! to you,

Whose star-like nobleness gave life and influence 68

To their whole being! I am rapt, and cannot cover

The monstrous bulk of this ingratitude

With any size of words.

    Tim. Let it go naked, men may see 't the bet-

        ter: 72

You, that are honest, by being what you are,

Make them best seen and known.

    Pain.   He and myself

Have travail'd in the great shower of your gifts,

49 black-corner'd; *cf. n.*   59 Fit: *it is fitting that*
69 rapt: *beside myself*

And sweetly felt it.

    Tim.   Ay, you are honest men.   76

    Pain. We are hither come to offer you our service.

    Tim. Most honest men! Why, how shall I requite
you?

Can you eat roots, and drink cold water? no.

    Both. What we can do, we'll do, to do you ser-
vice.   80

    Tim. Ye're honest men: ye've heard that I have
gold;

I am sure you have: speak truth; ye're honest men.

    Pain. So it is said, my noble lord: but therefore

Came not my friend nor I.   84

    Tim. Good honest men! Thou draw'st a counter-
feit

Best in all Athens: thou'rt indeed the best;

Thou counterfeit'st most lively.

    Pain.   So, so, my lord.

    Tim. E'en so, sir, as I say. And, for thy fic-
tion,   88

Why, thy verse swells with stuff so fine and smooth

That thou art even natural in thine art.

But for all this, my honest-natur'd friends,

I must needs say you have a little fault: 92

Marry, 'tis not monstrous in you; neither wish I

You take much pains to mend.

    Both.   Beseech your honour

To make it known to us.

    Tim.   You'll take it ill.

    Both. Most thankfully, my lord.

    Tim.   Will you, indeed?   96

    Both. Doubt it not, worthy lord.

    Tim. There's never a one of you but trusts a knave

85 counterfeit: *likeness*   87 lively: *to the life*
90 natural: *pun on 'natural,' a fool*

That mightily deceives you.

   Both.   Do we, my lord?

   Tim. Ay, and you hear him cog, see him dis-
semble,   100

Know his gross patchery, love him, feed him,

Keep in your bosom: yet remain assur'd

That he's a made-up villain.

   Pain. I know none such, my lord.

   Poet.   Nor I.   104

   Tim. Look you, I love you well; I'll give you gold,

Rid me these villains from your companies:

Hang them or stab them, drown them in a draught,

Confound them by some course, and come to me,   108

I'll give you gold enough.

   Both. Name them, my lord, let's know them.

   Tim. You that way, and you this, but two in company:

Each man apart, all single and alone,   112

Yet an arch-villain keeps him company.

If, where thou art two villains shall not be,

Come not near him. [*To the Poet.*] If thou would'st
not reside

But where one villain is, then him abandon.   116

Hence, pack! there's gold; you came for gold, ye
slaves:

[*To Painter.*] You have done work for me, there's
payment: hence!

[*To Poet.*] You are an alchemist, make gold of
that:

Out, rascal dogs!   120

   [*Beats them out, and then returns into his cave.*]

100 cog: *cheat*   101 patchery: *roguery*
103 made-up: *consummate*   107 draught: *cesspool*
117 pack: *depart*

Enter Steward [Flavius], and two Senators.

Flav. It is in vain that you would speak with
        Timon;
For he is set so only to himself
That nothing but himself which looks like man,
Is friendly with him.

 First Sen.   Bring us to his cave: 124
It is our part and promise to the Athenians
To speak with Timon.

 Sec. Sen.   At all times alike
Men are not still the same: 'twas time and griefs
That fram'd him thus: time, with his fairer hand, 128
Offering the fortunes of his former days,
The former man may make him. Bring us to him,
And chance it as it may.

 Flav.   Here is his cave.
Peace and content be here! Lord Timon! Timon! 132
Look out, and speak to friends. The Athenians,
By two of their most reverend senate, greet thee:
Speak to them, noble Timon.

Enter Timon out of his Cave.

 Tim. Thou sun, that comfort'st, burn! Speak, and
        be hang'd: 136
For each true word, a blister! and each false
Be as a cauterizing to the root o' the tongue,
Consuming it with speaking!

 First Sen.   Worthy Timon,—
 Tim. Of none but such as you, and you of
        Timon. 140
 Sec. Sen. The senators of Athens greet thee,
        Timon.

122 set . . . to himself: *wrapped up in himself*
125 part: *particular business*   128 fram'd: *moulded*
130 The . . . him: *may restore him to his former self*

Tim. I thank them, and would send them back the
  plague,
Could I but catch it for them.
  First Sen.   O, forget
What we are sorry for ourselves in thee.   144
The senators with one consent of love
Entreat thee back to Athens; who have thought
On special dignities, which vacant lie
For thy best use and wearing.
  Sec. Sen.   They confess   148
Toward thee forgetfulness too general, gross;
Which now the public body, which doth seldom
Play the recanter, feeling in itself
A lack of Timon's aid, hath sense withal   152
Of it own fail, restraining aid to Timon;
And send forth us, to make their sorrow'd render,
Together with a recompense more fruitful
Than their offence can weigh down by the dram;   156
Ay, even such heaps and sums of love and wealth,
As shall to thee blot out what wrongs were theirs,
And write in thee the figures of their love,
Ever to read them thine.
  Tim.   You witch me in it.   160
Surprise me to the very brink of tears:
Lend me a fool's heart and a woman's eyes,
And I'll beweep these comforts, worthy senators.
  First Sen. Therefore so please thee to return with
  us,   164
And of our Athens—thine and ours—to take
The captainship, thou shalt be met with thanks,
Allow'd with absolute power, and thy good name

152 hath . . . withal: *has, besides, a realization*
153 it: *its*   fail: *offence*
154 sorrow'd render: *confession of sorrow*
160 witch: *bewitch*   167 Allow'd: *sanctioned*

Live with authority: so soon we shall drive back   168
Of Alcibiades the approaches wild;
Who, like a boar too savage, doth root up
His country's peace.

   Sec. Sen.   And shakes his threat'ning sword
Against the walls of Athens.

    First Sen.   Therefore, Timon,—   172

    Tim. Well, sir, I will; therefore, I will, sir;
    thus:—
If Alcibiades kill my countrymen,
Let Alcibiades know this of Timon,
That Timon cares not. But if he sack fair
    Athens,   176
And take our goodly aged men by the beards,
Giving our holy virgins to the stain
Of contumelious, beastly, mad-brain'd war;
Then let him know, and tell him Timon speaks it,   180
In pity of our aged and our youth
I cannot choose but tell him, that I care not,
And let him take 't at worst; for their knives care not
While you have throats to answer: for myself   184
There's not a whittle in the unruly camp
But I do prize it at my love before
The reverend'st throat in Athens. So I leave you
To the protection of the prosperous gods,   188
As thieves to keepers.

   Flav.   Stay not; all's in vain.

   Tim. Why, I was writing of my epitaph;
It will be seen to-morrow. My long sickness
Of health and living now begins to mend,   192
And nothing brings me all things. Go, live still;
Be Alcibiades your plague, you his,

185 whittle: *small clasp-knife*   188 prosperous: *propitious*
193 nothing: *oblivion, death*

And last so long enough!
>   *First Sen.*   We speak in vain.
>   *Tim.* But yet I love my country, and am not   196
One that rejoices in the common wrack,
As common bruit doth put it.
>   *First Sen.*   That's well spoke.
>   *Tim.* Commend me to my loving countrymen,—
>   *First Sen.* These words become your lips as they
>   pass through them.   200
>   *Sec. Sen.* And enter in our ears like great triumph-
>   ers
In their applauding gates.
>   *Tim.*   Commend me to them;
And tell them, that, to ease them of their griefs,
Their fears of hostile strokes, their aches, losses,   204
Their pangs of love, with other incident throes
That nature's fragile vessel doth sustain
In life's uncertain voyage, I will some kindness do
>   them:
I'll teach them to prevent wild Alcibiades' wrath.   208
>   *Sec. Sen.* I like this well; he will return again.
>   *Tim.* I have a tree, which grows here in my close,
That mine own use invites me to cut down,
And shortly must I fell it: tell my friends,   212
Tell Athens, in the sequence of degree,
From high to low throughout, that whoso please
To stop affliction, let him take his haste,
Come hither, ere my tree hath felt the axe,   216
And hang himself. I pray you, do my greeting.
>   *Flav.* Trouble him no further; thus you still shall
>   find hin

197 wrack: *ruin*   198 bruit: *rumor*
208 prevent: *escape*   210 close: *enclosure*
213 in . . . degree: *one after another according to rank*
215 take . . . haste: *make haste*

Tim. Come not to me again; but say to Athens,
Timon hath made his everlasting mansion   220
Upon the beached verge of the salt flood;
Who once a day with his embossed froth
The turbulent surge shall cover: thither come,
And let my grave-stone be your oracle.   224
Lips, let sour words go by and language end:
What is amiss plague and infection mend!
Graves only be men's works and death their gain!
Sun, hide thy beams! Timon hath done his reign. 228

         Exit Timon.

First Sen. His discontents are unremovably
Coupled to nature.

  Sec. Sen. Our hope in him is dead: let us return,
And strain what other means is left unto us   232
In our dear peril.

  First Sen. It requires swift foot. *Exeunt.*

Scene Two

[Before the Walls of Athens]

Enter two other Senators, with a Messenger.

First Sen. Thou hast painfully discover'd: are his
 files
As full as thy report?

  Mess.   I have spoke the least:
Besides, his expedition promises
Present approach.   4

  Sec. Sen. We stand much hazard, if they bring not
 Timon.

  Mess. I met a courier, one mine ancient friend,

---

222 embossed: *foaming*   232 strain: *exert to the utmost*
1 painfully discover'd: *told distressing tidings* files: *ranks*

Whom, though in general part we were oppos'd,
Yet our old love made a particular force,   8
And made us speak like friends: this man was riding
From Alcibiades to Timon's cave,
With letters of entreaty, which imported
His fellowship i' the cause against your city,   12
In part for his sake mov'd.
    First Sen.   Here come our brothers.

    Enter the other Senators [from Timon].

    Third Sen. No talk of Timon, nothing of him
    expect.
The enemies' drum is heard, and fearful scouring
Doth choke the air with dust. In, and prepare: 16
Ours is the fall, I fear, our foes the snare.
                              Exeunt.

Scene Three

[The Woods. Timon's Cave, and a rude Tomb seen]

    Enter a Soldier in the Woods, seeking Timon.

    Sold. By all description this should be the place.
Who's here? speak, ho! No answer! What is this?
Timon is dead, who hath outstretch'd his span:
Some beast read this; there does not live a man.   4
Dead, sure; and this his grave. What's on this tomb
I cannot read; the character I'll take with wax:
Our captain hath in every figure skill,
An ag'd interpreter, though young in days.   8
Before proud Athens he's set down by this,
Whose fall the mark of his ambition is.   *Exit.*

---

7 in general part: *in the public cause*
3 outstretch'd his span: *reached the limit of his life*
4 read; *cf. n.*   6 character: *writing*

Scene Four

[*Before the Walls of Athens*]

*Trumpets sound.   Enter Alcibiades with his Powers
before Athens.*

Alcib. Sound to this coward and lascivious town
Our terrible approach.   *Sounds a parley.*

The Senators appear upon the Walls.

Till now you have gone on and fill'd the time
With all licentious measure, making your wills   4
The scope of justice; till now myself and such
As slept within the shadow of your power
Have wander'd with our travers'd arms, and breath'd
Our sufferance vainly. Now the time is flush,   8
When crouching marrow, in the bearer strong,
Cries of itself, 'No more:' now breathless wrong
Shall sit and pant in your great chairs of ease,
And pursy insolence shall break his wind   12
With fear and horrid flight.
    First Sen.   Noble and young,
When thy first griefs were but a mere conceit,
Ere thou hadst power or we had cause of fear,
We sent to thee, to give thy rages balm,   16
To wipe out our ingratitude with loves
Above their quantity.
    Sec. Sen.   So did we woo
Transformed Timon to our city's love
By humble message and by promis'd means: 20
We were not all unkind, nor all deserve
The common stroke of war.

7 travers'd arms: *folded arms, reversed arms* (?)
8 flush: *full*   9 marrow: *vigor*
12 pursy: *short-winded*   14 griefs: *grievances*   conceit: *fancy*
20 promis'd means: *means of promises* (?)

First Sen.   These walls of ours
Were not erected by their hands from whom
You have receiv'd your grief: nor are they such   24
That these great towers, trophies, and schools should
    fall
For private faults in them.
Sec. Sen.   Nor are they living
Who were the motives that you first went out;
Shame that they wanted cunning in excess   28
Hath broke their hearts.   March, noble lord,
Into our city with thy banners spread:
By decimation, and a tithed death,—
If thy revenges hunger for that food   32
Which nature loathes,—take thou the destin'd tenth,
And by the hazard of the spotted die
Let die the spotted.
First Sen.   All have not offended;
For those that were, it is not square to take,   36
On those that are, revenges: crimes like lands
Are not inherited.   Then, dear countryman,
Bring in thy ranks, but leave without thy rage:
Spare thy Athenian cradle and those kin   40
Which, in the bluster of thy wrath, must fall
With those that have offended: like a shepherd,
Approach the fold and cull th' infected forth,
But kill not all together.
Sec. Sen.   What thou wilt,   44
Thou rather shalt enforce it with thy smile
Than hew to 't with thy sword.
First Sen.   Set but thy foot
Against our rampir'd gates, and they shall ope,

27 motives: *agents*   28 that . . . excess: *at their excessive folly*
31 tithed: *involving the slaughter of a tenth*
35 spotted: *stained*   36 square: *proper*
39 without: *outside*   46 hew to 't: *cut the way to it*
47 rampir'd: *fortified against an attack*

So thou wilt send thy gentle heart before,   48
To say thou'lt enter friendly.
    Sec. Sen.   Throw thy glove,
Or any token of thine honour else,
That thou wilt use the wars as thy redress
And not as our confusion, all thy powers   52
Shall make their harbour in our town, till we
Have seal'd thy full desire.
    Alcib.   Then there's my glove;
Descend, and open your uncharged ports:
Those enemies of Timon's and mine own,   56
Whom you yourselves shall set out for reproof,
Fall, and no more: and, to atone your fears
With my more noble meaning, not a man
Shall pass his quarter, or offend the stream   60
Of regular justice in your city's bounds,
But shall be render'd to your public laws
At heaviest answer.
    Both.   'Tis most nobly spoken.
    Alcib. Descend, and keep your words.   64
    [*The Senators descend, and open the gates.*]

           Enter a Messenger.

    Mess. My noble-general, Timon is dead;
Entomb'd upon the very hem o' the sea;
And on his grave-stone this insculpture, which
With wax I brought away, whose soft impression   68
Interprets for my poor ignorance.

      Alcibiades reads the epitaph.

48 So: *if only*   54 seal'd: *brought to completion*
55 uncharged: *unattacked*   ports: *gates*
58 atone: *set at one*   60 quarter: *lodging place*
62 render'd: *surrendered*   63 At . . . answer: *to pay the full penalty*
67 insculpture: *carved inscription*

Alcib. 'Here lies a wretched corse, of wretched soul
    bereft:
Seek not my name: a plague consume you wicked
    caitiffs left!
Here lie I, Timon; who, alive, all living men did
    hate: 72
Pass by, and curse thy fill; but pass and stay not here
    thy gait.'
These well express in thee thy latter spirits:
Though thou abhorr'dst in us our human griefs,
Scorn'dst our brain's flow and those our droplets
    which   76
From niggard nature fall, yet rich conceit
Taught thee to make vast Neptune weep for aye
On thy low grave, on faults forgiven. Dead
Is noble Timon, of whose memory   80
Hereafter more. Bring me into your city,
And I will use the olive with my sword,
Make war breed peace, make peace stint war, make
    each
Prescribe to other as each other's leech.   84
Let our drums strike.   *Exeunt.*

FINIS.

70-73 Here . . . gait; *cf. n.*   70 corse: *corpse*
76 brain's flow: *tears*   83 stint: *stop*   84 leech: *physician*

NOTES

Dramatis Personæ. In the First Folio the last page of Timon of Athens bears the caption: 'The Actors' Names.' Additions to this list of characters have been placed in brackets. In the Folio Sempronius' name occurs twice. Ventidius is known as Ventigius; Philotus as Philo; and Hortensius as Hortensis. See the facsimile frontispiece to this volume.

I. i. S. d. *Enter . . . and Mercer.* The stage direction of the Folio has been restored. Many modern editors have changed it to read: *Enter . . . Merchant, and others . . . ,* omitting the 'Mercer.' Whether or not the 'Mercer' speaks during the scene is not made clear by the text of the Folio, since each speech is preceded by *Mer.,* which may represent, equally well, either 'Merchant' or 'Mercer.'

I. i. 3. *It wears, sir, as it grows.* A half-facetious reply to the Poet's greeting: as the world grows older it wears away.

I. i. 15. *'When we for recompense,'* etc. A stage direction might be added: 'Reciting to himself,' or 'Reading from his poems.'

I. i. 23-25. *our gentle flame . . . chafes.* The poet's fancy is self-inspired, and, like a swift stream, it flies away from every boundary which it chafes. 'Bound' refers to the banks of the stream; against these the current 'chafes,' but speeds onward.

I. i. 27. *Upon the heels of my presentment, sir.* 'As soon as my book has been presented to Lord Timon.' (Johnson.) In Shakespeare's day, as later, the success of a book often depended upon its patron.

I. i. 31, 32. *how this grace Speaks his own stand-*

ing! How truly the gracefulness of this figure expresses the dignity of the original!

I. i. 34, 35. *to the dumbness of the gesture One might interpret.* To the mute eloquence of this gesture one might easily supply words. This line may allude to the 'interpreter' whose function was to explain the action of the puppet-shows. Cf. *Hamlet*, III. ii. 260, 261.

I. i. 48. *In a wide sea of wax.* The usual explanation that reference is made to use among the ancients of writing-tablets covered with wax, is not wholly satisfactory.

I. i. 48-51. *no levell'd malice . . . behind.* 'Shakespeare's meaning is, my poem is not a satire written with any particular view, or levelled at any single person; I fly like an eagle into the general expanse of life, and leave not, by any private mischief, the trace of my passage.' (Johnson.) Keightley conjectures that a lacuna exists after 'hold.'

I. i. 77, 78. *would . . . condition.* 'Would find a striking parallel in our state.' (Schmidt.) Of various interpretations this seems most convincing. However, it is possible that by 'condition' the painter means 'art'; specifically, 'the art of painting.'

I. i. 96. *five talents.* About six thousand dollars. A talent was approximately twelve hundred dollars.

I. i. 129-132. *The man is honest . . . daughter.* 'The meaning of the first line the poet himself explains, or rather unfolds, in the second. "The man is honest!"—True; and for that very cause, and with no additional or extrinsic motive, he will be so. No man can be justly called honest, who is not so for honesty's sake, itself including its reward.' (Coleridge.)

I. i. 166. *Hath . . . dispraise.* Timon's statement that the jewel has been embarrassingly praised

or valued is misunderstood by the jeweller; he interprets 'under praise' as 'dispraise.'

I. i. 170. *As . . . give.* At a figure which those
who sell would be willing to pay.

I. i. 181. *When . . , honest.* Until you become a
dog and these knaves become honest,—remote con-
tingencies!

I. i. 217. *plain-dealing.* An allusion to the proverb, 'Plain-dealing is a jewel, but they that use it die
beggars.'

I. i. 242. *That I had no angry wit to be a lord.*
It is possible that the adjective 'angry' is corrupt. As
it stands in the text the line seems to express the
annoyance of Apemantus at the idea that angry self-
derision should not be aroused in him at the fact of
his being a lord.

I. i. 258. *Aches.* To be scanned as a dissyllable.

I. i. 288. *Plutus, the god of gold.* The Greek per-
sonification of riches. He was supposed to have been
blinded by Zeus so that he might distribute his gifts
without choice.

I. ii. 21, 22. *confess'd . . . not.* In all likelihood
an allusion to the proverb of Shakespeare's time:
'Confess and be hanged.'

I. ii. 28-44. *They say . . . too.* It is difficult to
state whether these lines, and others in the play,
should be printed as poetry or as prose. Certain
modern editors give them as prose.

I. ii. 28. *'Ira furor brevis est.'* Wrath is a brief
madness. Horace, *Epistles,* Book I. ii. 62.

I. ii. 46. *Methinks they should invite them without
knives.* The Elizabethan guests were accustomed to
bring their knives to feasts. (Ritson.)

I. ii. 111, 112. *O joy, . . . born.* Timon's tears
of joy choke and seem to belie the very happiness that
provokes them.

I. ii. 115, 116. *Thou weep'st to make them drink,*

Timon. The tears you shed so bountifully would be
a suitable beverage for the flatterers (rather than the
wine they swill). Or, perhaps, the remark is merely
a sneer at the incongruity of Timon's weeping while
his guests drink.

I. ii. 129 S. d. *Enter Cupid.* I.e., the 'forerunner,' a boy dressed to personate the god of love;
as in *As You Like It,* V. iv, one personates Hymen,
the god of marriage.

I. ii. 138 S. d. *with the masque of Ladies [as]*
Amazons. The masque, a form of histrionic spec-
tacle, was much in vogue during the early seventeenth
century. There are masque-like features in *Henry*
VIII, The Winter's Tale, and *The Tempest,* all written within a few years of *Timon of Athens.* No stage
direction occurs at this point in the Folio. Instead,
the words clearly required here are by anticipation
added to the stage directions after lines 121 and 129.
The former reads: 'Sound Tucket. Enter the Maskers of Amazons, with Lutes in their hands, dauncing
and playing;' and the latter: 'Enter Cupid with the
Maske of Ladies.'

I. ii. 140. *they are mad women.* This line may
reflect the Puritan spirit of the time. Stubbes'
Anatomie of Abuses (1583), speaks of 'Dauncers
thought to be madmen.' 'There were (saith Ludovi-
cus Vives) from far countries certain men brought
into our parts of the world, who, when they saw men
daunce, ran away marvellously affraid, crying out and
thinking them mad.'

I. ii. 141, 142. *Like madness . . . root.* 'Just
such madness is the glory of this life as the pomp of
this feast appears when compared with the philosopher's frugal repast of a little oil and a few roots.'
(Clarke.)

I. ii. 152. *Men shut their doors against a setting*
sun. A proverbial saying, the sense of which is illus-

trated by a passage in Bacon's essay on Friendship
(1625): 'L. Sylla, when he commanded Rome, raised
Pompey, after surnamed the Great, to that height,
that Pompey vaunted himself for Sylla's over-match.
For when he had the consulship for a friend of his
against the pursuit of Sylla, and that Sylla did a
little resent thereat, and began to speak great, Pompey turned upon him again, and in effect bade him be
quiet; for that more men adored the sun rising, than
the sun setting.'

I. ii. 170. *When all . . . could.* There is a quibble on 'cross'd,' and 'crossing' in line 168. 'Cross'd'
probably refers to the cross upon many coins of the
day. Hence, 'to be crossed' or 'to bear a cross' was
a joking expression meaning 'to have ready cash.' Or
the quibble may refer to the crossing out of a debt on
the creditor's books.

I. ii. 171, 172. *'Tis pity . . . mind.* In order that
bounty might be able to foresee the evils and miseries
about to attack it.

I. ii. 187. The meaning is illustrated by a parallel
passage in *Julius Cæsar,* III. i. 6-8:

'O Cæsar, read mine first; for mine's a suit
That touches Cæsar nearer . . .

Cæs. What touches us ourself shall be last serv'd.'

I. ii. 226. *I'll call to you.* Sandys in the *Shakespeare Society Papers* (vol. iii., p. 23), says that the
expression 'I'll call *to* (i.e., *at*) your house' is still
(1846) employed in the West of England.

I. ii. 234. *defil'd.* Used here with a play on
'pitch'd.' Cf. *Henry IV., Part 1,* II. iv. 460, 461:
'Pitch . . . doth defile.'

I. ii. 241. *legs.* Used here with a play upon the
two senses of 'limbs' and 'bowings.'

I. ii. 255. *come . . . music.* 'Come again in a
better tone of mind.'

II. i. 10. *No porter at his gate.* In Elizabethan days the porter was a stern guardian. Cf. Thomas Dekker's *A Knight's Conjuring:* 'You mistake, if you imagine that Plutoe's *porter* is like one of those big fellows that stand like gyants at lordes gates.'

II. i. 30, 31. *When every feather . . . gull.* When every creditor has his proper due, Lord Timon will be stripped. 'Gull' is used with a play upon the meanings of 'unfledged bird' and 'dupe.'

II. ii. 5, 6. *never . . . kind.* Never was mind made to be so unwise, and yet so kind.

II. ii. 9, 11. *Varro . . . Isidore.* The servants are addressed by their masters' names.

II. ii. 14. *we'll forth again.* It was an Elizabethan custom to hunt both before and after dinner. While at Kenilworth Castle Queen Elizabeth hunted afternoons.

II. ii. 57. *No, thou . . . yet.* When Apemantus says 'thou' he speaks to the servant of Varro; 'thou'rt' is addressed to the servant of Isidore.

II. ii. 94. *to Lord Timon's.* Almost certainly an error if this scene is laid in Timon's house. Perhaps, however, the action occurs in the street outside.

II. ii. 117. *philosopher,* etc. The 'philosopher's stone' or 'great elixir' was, in alchemy, a soluble, solid substance supposed to have the property of transmuting baser metals into silver or gold, and of prolonging life. Cf. *Henry IV, Part 2,* III. ii. 355.

II. ii. 153. *yet now's a time.* Flavius means that, although too late to save Timon, there is at least an opportunity now to acquaint him with true conditions.

II. ii. 165. *If . . . falsehood.* Zeugma makes the line awkward. Flavius means: 'If you question my thrift or suspect me of falsehood.'

II. ii. 207, 208. *Of whom . . . hearing.* 'By whom, by reason of my previous services, I expect my request ('hearing') to be honored, even to the extent of the State's fullest resources.'

III. i. 51. *And we alive that liv'd?* In this brief
time. 'That we, who only yesterday saw Timon's
friends at his feet, should to-day see them spurning
him after this man's fashion.'

III. i. 56. *Let molten coin be thy damnation.*

'And ladles full of melted gold
Were poured down their throats.'
—Old Ballad, '*The Dead Man's Song.*'

Possibly the allusion is to the fate of Marcus Crassus,
down whose throat the Parthians poured melted gold.

III. ii. 52-54. *that I . . . honour.* Of the many
explanations of this passage that of Steevens is the
best: 'By purchasing what brought me little honour,
I have lost the more honourable opportunity of supplying the wants of my friend.'

III. iii. 12. *Thrice.* Johnson's reading. The
Folio has 'Thriue,' which some modern editors have
adopted. In such a case the allusion would be to the
rich and indifferent physician who flourishes at the
expense of his patient. Cf. Webster, *Duchess of
Malfi*, III. v. 7-9.

'physicians thus,
With their hands full of money use to give o'er
Their patients.'

III. iii. 28-31. *The devil . . . clear.* The devil
did not appreciate the significance of making man
politic. By it he defeated his own purpose, for the
villainies of man will, by comparison, make him
appear innocent.

III. iv. 13. *Is like the sun's.* 'Like him in blaze
and splendour.' (Johnson.)

III. iv. 92. *Knock me down with 'em,* etc. A
quibble upon 'bills' in the sense of weapons (i.e., a
kind of long-handled axe).

III. iv. 105 S. d. *Enter Timon [and Flavius].* This
represents the modern editors' conception of the action.

According to the Folio, Flavius does not leave the stage at line 60, and Timon, reentering at the present point, finds him still there.

III. iv. 114. *Sempronius: all.* In the First Folio this portion of the line reads: *Sempronius Vllorxa: All.* Of the many conjectures concerning this puzzling corruption the least improbable seems to be that 'Vllorxa' is a printer's error for the name of another character, possibly Ventidius.

III. v. 49. *if bearing carry it.* 'If endurance is the greater virtue.'

III. v. 50. *fellow.* As in the First Folio. Johnson's plausible reading is 'felon.'

III. v. 107. *Only in bone . . . you.* 'That you may live to be mere skeletons, and scare men from looking at you.' (Clarke.)

III. v. 117. *lay for hearts.* 'Endeavour to win popular affection.' (Clarke.)

III. vi. 5. *tiring.* 'A metaphorical application of the language of falconry, in which a hawk was said to tire upon the refuse of her prey, which the falconer threw to her as reward and encouragement.' 'An hawke Tyryth upon rumpes. She fedyth on all manere of flesshe. She gorgith whan she fyllyth her gorge wyth meete.' (The boke of hawkynge, huntyng, and fysshynge by Juliana Berners, ciij.)

III. vi. 38, 39. *if they will fare . . . sound.* If the anticipated trumpet signal is so harshly delayed. Dinner was announced in great households by the sounding of trumpets. Cf. *Othello,* IV. ii. 169.

III. vi. 108. *minute-jacks.* Contemptible fellows who change their minds every minute. It is possible that the word has reference to the 'Jacks-of-the-Clock,' figures that struck the bells in the old clocks.

III. vi. 131. *stones.* There is no evidence in this play that stones were thrown at the guests. In the old play, *Timon,* stones are painted to resemble artichokes and are hurled at the parasites. It is possible

that this line is reminiscent of the older play. See
Appendix A, pp. 113, 114, and 115.

IV. ii. 35. *and all what state compounds*. 'All
that goes to make up state.'

IV. iii. 9. *Raise me . . . lord*. 'Give elevation to
a beggar, but deny it to a lord.'

IV. iii. 12. *rother's*. Singer's emendation for
'Brothers' of the Folio. Holloway's *General Provin-
cial Dictionary* mentions the 'rother market' of Strat-
ford-on-Avon. The sentence, as printed in the Folio
runs: 'It is the Pastour Lards, the Brothers sides,
The want that makes him leaue.'

IV. iii. 27. *idle votarist*. Timon means, presum-
ably: '*My* vows of hate for human wealth are not
insincere. The discovery of gold will not send me
back to the life I have forsworn.'

IV. iii. 32. *Pluck . . . heads*. An old custom of
drawing away the pillows of dying men to render
their deaths easier, and, sometimes, for the inhuman
purpose of hastening their departures.

IV. iii. 44. *Do thy right nature*. 'Lie in the earth
where nature laid thee.' (Johnson.)

IV. iii. 53. *'Misanthropos.'* North's Plutarch has
this marginal note: 'Antonius followeth the life and
example of Timon Misanthropos, the Athenian.'

IV. iii. 87. *To the tub-fast and the diet*. An allusion to the sweating cure used by the Elizabethans.

IV. iii. 109. *planetary plague*. A reference to a
common belief of the time that plagues and pesti-
lences were often due to the malignant influence of
the planets. Cf. *King Lear*, I. ii. 139, 140: 'By an
enforced obedience of planetary influence.' Cf. also
Troilus and Cressida, I. iii. 94-96:

> 'but when the planets
> In evil mixture to disorder wander,
> What plagues and what portents! . . .'

IV. iii. 134, 135. *Enough . . . bawd.* 'Enough
to make a whore leave whoring, and a bawd leave
making whores.' (Johnson.)

IV. iii. 145, 146. *and thatch . . . dead.* 'Cover
your thin heads with false hair taken from dead
bodies.' Shakespeare repeatedly attacks the practice
of wearing false hair.

IV. iii. 185. *Hyperion.* A Titan, the father of
Helios, the sun-god. The name is used here, as elsewhere, for the sun itself.

IV. iii. 232. *Answer mere nature.* 'Cope with
nature in all its stark rigour.' (Deighton.) Cf.
King Lear, III. iv. 104: 'Answer with thy uncovered
body this extremity of the skies.'

IV. iii. 238, 239. *Always . . . too.* Timon means
that to vex another is the function of a fool or a villain. He has hitherto thought of Apemantus as a
fool; Apemantus' 'Ay' leads him to think him also a
knave, or villain.

IV. iii. 253, 254. *proceeded . . . degrees.* Technical terms used at English universities.

IV. iii. 255. *drudges.* Mason's reading for
'drugges.' The New English Dictionary, quoting
Huloet (1552) says: 'Drudge, or *drugge,* or vile servant in a house, whych doth all the vyle service.'

IV. iii. 286, 287. *'Tis not . . . would it were.*
'Even then (when mended by lack of *my* company)
your company, being the company of yourself alone,
cannot be said to be *well* mended, but only to be
clumsily patched, a mere piece of botchery; if not,
I wish you might find it so.'

IV. iii. 288. *What . . . Athens.* What commission do you wish to give me for Athens?

IV. iii. 305. *medlar.* The fruit of the tree Mespi-
lus Germanica, which is like a small brown-skinned
apple and is eaten when in a soft, pulpy state. It
is used in this passage, as elsewhere in Shakespeare,
with a pun upon the word 'meddler.'

IV. iii. 312. *after his means.* 'After' may have the significance of 'according to,' or the phrase may mean: 'after his means are gone.'

IV. iii. 339. *wert thou the unicorn,* etc. 'It was supposed that unicorns, in their fury, would rush at their enemy blindly, strike their horn against a tree, stick fast, and so be killed.' Cf. *Julius Cæsar,* II. i. 204: 'Unicorns may be betray'd with trees.'

IV. iii. 344-346. *wert thou . . . life.* If you were a leopard, you would be akin to the lion, and your spots would be the cause of your death. The line alludes to the jealousy of the lion, which tolerates no rival.

IV. iii. 358. *Yonder comes a poet and a painter.* This mistake is typical of the confused text of the play. The poet and the painter do not enter until the next act. See Appendix C, p. 126, footnote 4.

IV. iii. 386. *Hymen.* The Greek god of marriage and of the marriage song named after him.

IV. iii. 445, 446. *whose liquid . . . tears.* Alluding to the influence of the moon upon the tides. There existed, too, a popular belief that the moon influenced the weather. In *Hamlet* (I. i. 118), the moon is called the 'moist star.'

IV. iii. 475, 476. *How rarely . . . enemies.* 'How admirably does the injunction to love one's enemies accord with the fashion of the times!' (Rolfe.)

IV. iii. 477, 478. *Grant . . . that do.* 'Let me rather *woo* or caress those that *would* mischief, that *profess to mean me mischief,* than those that *really do me mischief* under false professions of kindness.' (Johnson.) Cf. the Spanish proverb: 'Defend me from my friends, and from my enemies I will defend myself.'

V. i. 49. *black-corner'd night.* 'Night shrouding all with the darkness of black corners.'

V. iii. 4. *read.* The Folio reading. Warburton

suggested 'rear'd,' implying that the rude tomb could not have been erected by man. If 'read' is accepted two interpretations are possible: (1) The line may be part of an inscription on the tomb, or (2) it may be a contemptuous comment from the soldier: 'Let a beast read this; there is no man present who can do so!'

V. iv. 70-73. *Here . . . gait.* These lines are a combination of two epitaphs, both appearing in North's Plutarch. Lines 71 and 72 are clearly contradictory. See Appendix A, pp. 110 and 111.

APPENDIX A

SOURCES OF THE PLAY

The basic legend of Shakespeare's *Timon of Athens* began in antiquity. Early in the fifth century B. C., Timon's picturesque misanthropy was a theme of Greek comic poets. The hero of *The Misanthrope*, by Phrynichus, remarks: 'I live like Timon. I have no wife, no servant, I am irritable and hard to get on with. I never laugh, I never talk, and my opinions are all my own.' From the uncertain realms of casual allusion emerge two later Greek portrayals of the character of Timon: The story of the misanthrope in Plutarch's *Life of Antonius*, and Lucian's comic dialogue, *Timon the Misanthrope*.[1]

How much Plutarch had already yielded Shakespeare we know; here were the geneses of *Julius Cæsar, Coriolanus,* and *Antony and Cleopatra*. And if it is believed that *Timon of Athens* was written at about the same time as the last-named tragedy, it is conceivable that the full possibilities of the Timon legend were brought home to Shakespeare in the very act of composing *Antony and Cleopatra*. The dramatist's reliance upon this source is suggested by the following excerpt: '*Antonius,* he forsooke the citie and

[1] Definite references to Timon occur in the comedies of Aristophanes, Plato, and Antiphanes. He is later mentioned by Roman writers, notably Cicero, Seneca, the Elder Pliny, and Strabo. Strabo was the first to allude to Timon's early life of affluence. It is quite certain that the legend had general currency. For full compilations of classical and Elizabethan allusions to the Timon story the reader is referred to Dr. Ernest Hunter Wright's monograph, *The Authorship of Timon of Athens,* Columbia University Press, 1910, and W. H. Clemons' *The Sources of Timon of Athens,* in the Princeton University Bulletin, September, 1904.

companie of his friends, and built him a house in the
sea, & dwelt there, as a man that banished himself
from all mens company: saying that he would leade
Timons life because he had the like wrong offered
him, that was before offered vnto *Timon:* and that for
the vnthankfulnesse of those he had done good vnto,
and whom he tooke to be his friends, he was angrie
with all men, and would trust no man. This *Timon*
was a citizen of ATHENS, that liued about the war
of PELOPONNESUS, as appeareth by *Plato* & *Aristophanes* comedies: in the which they mocked him,
calling him a viper and malicious man vnto mankind,
to shun all other mens companies, but the companie
of young *Alcibiades,* a bold and insolent youth, whom
he would greatly feast and make much of, and kissed
him very gladly. *Apemantus* wondering at it, asked
him the cause what he meant to make so much of that
young man alone, and to hate all others: *Timon*
answered him, I do it, said he, because I know that
one day he shall do great mischiefe vnto the ATHE-
NIANS.[1] This *Timon* sometimes would haue *Apemantus* in his companie, because he was much like of
his nature and conditions, and also followed him in
manner of life. On a time when they solemnly cele-
brated the feasts called Choæ at ATHENS, (to wit,
the feasts of the dead where they make sprinklings
and sacrifices for the dead) and that they two then
feasted together by them selues, *Apemantus* said vnto
the other: O here is a trim banquet *Timon.* *Timon*
answered again: Yea, said he, so thou wert not here.[2]
It is reported of him also, that this *Timon* on a time
(the people being assembled in the market place about
dispatch of some affaires) got vp into the pulpit for
Orations, where the Oratours commonly vse to speake

---

1 For Alcibiades' part in *Timon of Athens,* see III. v.;
IV. iii.; V. iv. Plutarch's *Life of Alcibiades* refers to him
as Timon's friend.

2 See *Timon of Athens,* IV. iii. 284 ff.

vnto the people: and silence being made, euery man
listening to heare what he would say, because it was
a wonder to see him in that place, at length he began
to speake in this manner: My Lords of ATHENS, I
haue a litle yard at my house where there groweth a
figge tree, on the which many citizens have hanged
themselues: and because I meane to make some build-
ing on the place, I thought good to let you all vnder-
stand it, that before the figge tree be cut downe, if
any of you be desperate, you may there in time go
hang your selues.[1] He died in the citie of HALES,
and was buried vpon the sea side. Now it chanced so,
that the sea getting in, compassed his tombe round
about, that no man could come to it: and vpon the
same was written this Epitaph:

Here lies a wretched corse, of wretched soule bereft:
Seeke not my name: a plague consume you wicked
    wretches left.

It is reported that *Timon* himselfe, when he liued,
made this Epitaph: for that which is commonly
rehearsed, was not his, but made by the Poet Calli-
machus:

Here lye I Timon, who aliue all liuing men did hate:
Passe by and curse thy fill: but passe, and stay not
    here thy gate.'

It will be observed that the themes of this ancient
story have been much expanded and enriched by
Shakespeare. The 'vnthankfulnesse of those he had
done good vnto,' elaborated, becomes the *motif* for
Timon's perversion; and 'young Alcibiades,' with his
hatred for Athens, dominates the underplot. Were
proof needed, the epitaphs show Shakespeare's dependence upon Plutarch. They are quoted in juxta-
position, but are contradictory. The inclusion of both

[1] For Shakespeare's use of the incident of the fig-tree, see
Timon of Athens, V. i. 210-217.

instead of the selection of one must be due to inadvertence or misunderstanding on the part of the poet. In fact, the more the passage in Plutarch is studied the more certainly does it appear that this or a later work based upon Plutarch, such as Painter's *Palace of Pleasure* (1566),[1] is the dynamic or inspirational source of our play.

Nevertheless, certain incidents can be attributed neither to Plutarch nor Painter. Of basic principles and ideas Plutarch is the source; for other episodes and character portraiture the responsibility is elsewhere. It is probable that one such source was an old Elizabethan comedy of Timon of Athens, acted about 1600. More or less faithful analogues may be found in the old play for the following incidents: Timon's betrayal by the parasites; the mock-banquet; Timon's exile; the finding of the gold; and, though less certainly, the episodes of the Old Athenian and Ventidius. Since these incidents occur also in Lucian's *Dialogues*,[2] such evidence proves only that Shake-

[1] The twenty-eighth novel of Painter's *Palace of Pleasure* is of *The strange and beastly nature of Timon of Athens*, based upon Plutarch, and adding only the particular that Timon lived in a desert. We know that the *Palace of Pleasure* furnished the source of *All's Well that Ends Well*, and that it influenced *Romeo and Juliet*. It is, accordingly, unlikely that Shakespeare was unfamiliar with the novel of *Timon of Athens*. The exact proportion of Shakespeare's reference, in writing the tragedy, to Plutarch or Painter is, of course, indeterminable. Perhaps the most reasonable conclusion concerning the matter is that he retained a general recollection of Painter, but that a copy of Plutarch lay before him as he wrote.

[2] The amount of Shakespeare's obligation to *Timon the Misanthrope* in Lucian's *Dialogues* has been rather widely disputed. When Shakespeare's play was written there existed no English translation of Lucian's *Dialogues*. Unless the tale of Shakespeare's Greek is discredited, he cannot be believed conversant with the original. If he was influenced it must have been through existent French or Italian translations. Shakespeare's tragedy includes no

speare drew either from one or both of these sources.
But the mock-banquet and the all-sacrificing steward
are to be found in the old play and *not* in Lucian.
In the portion of the old play's mock-banquet scene
here reprinted (IV. v.), the reader will find much in
substance and spirit worthy of comparison with the
corresponding scene in Shakespeare's play (III. vi.).

(Act IV, Scene v.)

Timon, Laches, Obba, Philargurus, Gelasimus,
Pseudocheus, Demeas, Eutrapelus: Hermogenes, Stilpo, Speusippus *come awhile after.*

Tim. Furnish the table, sette on dainty cheare;
Timon doth bidde his friends their last farewell.
  Phil. Thou wisely dost; it is too late to spare
When all is spent; whom the gods woulde haue
To liue but poorely, let him bee content.
  Tim. What man is hee can wayle the losse of
    wealthe,
Guarded with such a friendly company?
Ill thriue my gold, it shall not wring one teare
From these mine eies, nor one sigh from my hearte:
My friends sticke close to mee, they will not starte.
  Dem. Is hee madde? wee knew him not this
    morning:
Hath hee soe soone forgotte an iniury?

* * * * * * *

passages traceable to Lucian which cannot as readily be
ascribed to the old play or another source of later date than
Lucian. Yet the absence of evidence has failed to convince
certain critics that Shakespeare was not directly affected
by the *Dialogues.* 'The Timon of Shakespeare,' says W. H.
Clemons, 'is not the Timon of the academic production; still
less is it like the Timon of the popular Elizabethan stories.
In the depth and tone of his misanthropy, Lucian's Timon is
the true type of Shakespeare's Timon.' (Princeton University Bulletin, September, 1904, 219.) The same writer also
calls attention to the likeness in Timon's apostrophes to the
gold in Lucian and in Shakespeare (IV. iii. 25 ff.).

Enter TIMON

Tim. O happy mee, equall to Joue himselfe!
I going touche the starres. Breake out, O joy,
And smother not thyselfe within my breast!
Soe many friends, soe many friends I see;
Not one hathe falsifi'de his faith to mee.
What, if I am opprest with pouertie?
And griefe doth vexe mee? fortune left mee poore?
All this is nothing: they releeue my wants;
The one doth promise helpe, another golde,
A thirde a friendly welcome to his house
And entertainement; eache man actes his parte;
All promise counsaile and a faithfull hearte.

Gelas. Timon, thou art forgettefull of thy feast.

Tim. Why doe yee not fall to? I am at home:
Ile standing suppe, or walking, if I please.—
Laches, bring here the artichokes with speede.—
Eutrapelus, Demeas, Hermogenes,
I'le drinke this cuppe, a healthe to all your healths!

Lach. Conuerte it into poison, O ye gods!
Let it bee ratsbane to them!   [*Aside.*

Gelas. What, wilt thou haue the legge or els the
     winge?

Eutr. Carue yee that capon.

Dem. I will cutte him up,
And make a beaste of him.

Phil. Timon, this healthe to thee.

Tim. Ile pledge you, sir.
These artichokes doe noe mans pallat please.

Dem. I loue them well, by Joue.

Tim. Here, take them, then!
     [*Stones painted like to them; and throwes them
        at them.*
Nay, thou shalt haue them, thou and all of yee!
Yee wicked, base, perfidious rascalls,
Thinke yee my hate's soe soone extinguished?
     [TIMON *beates* HERM. *aboue all the reste.*

Dem. O my heade!

Herm. O my cheekes!

Phil. Is this a feaste?

Gelas. Truly, a stony one.

Stil. Stones sublunary haue the same matter with
the heauenly.

Tim. If I Ioues horridde thunderbolte did holde
Within my hande, thus, thus would I darte it!

                    [*He hitts* Herm.

Herm. Woe and alas, my braines are dashed out!

Gelas. Alas, alas, twill neuer bee my happe,
To trauaile now to the Antipodes!
Ah, that I had my Pegasus but here!
I'de fly away, by Ioue.

        [*Exeunt (all except* Tim. *and* Lach.)

Tim. Yee are a stony generation,
Or harder, if ought harder may bee founde;
Monsters of Scythia inhospitall,
Nay, very diuells, hatefull to the gods.

Lach. Master, they are gone.

Tim. The pox goe with them;
And whatsoe're the horridde sounding sea
Or earthe produces, whatsoe're accurs'd
Lurks in the house of silent Erebus,
Let it, O, let it all sprawl forth here! here,
Cocytus, flowe, and yee blacke foords of Styx!
Here barke thou, Cerberus! and here, yee troopes
Of cursed Furies, shake your firy brands!
Earth's worse than hell: let hell chaunge place with
earth,
And Plutoes regiment bee next the sunne!

Lach. Will this thy fury neuer bee appeas'd?

Tim. Neuer, neuer it; it will burne for euer:
It pleases mee to hate. Goe, Timon, goe,
Banishe thyselfe from mans society;
Farther than hell fly this inhumane city:
If there bee any exile to bee had,
There will I hide my heade.   [*Exit.*

Lach. Ile follow thee through sword, through fire,
  and deathe;
If thou goe to the ghosts, Ile bee thy page,
And lacky thee to the pale house of hell:
Thy misery shall make my faith excell.   [*Exit.*

Besides similarity of spirit in the two scenes, much
has been made of the possible reminiscence of Shakespeare's line: 'One day he gives us diamonds, next day
stones' (III. vi. 132). Shakespeare's use of the mock-
banquet and of the loyal steward, when no such
precedent exists in Lucian, argues strongly for his
dependence upon the old comedy of *Timon.* Steevens
and Malone believed in this indebtedness. Dyce, the
editor of the comedy, did not investigate the matter
deeply. 'I leave to others,' he says in his introduction, 'a minute discussion of the question, whether or
not Shakespeare was indebted to the present piece. I
shall merely observe, that I entertain considerable
doubts of his having been acquainted with a drama,
which was certainly never performed in the metropo-
lis, and which was likely to have been read only by a
few of the author's particular friends, to whom manu-
scripts of it had been presented.' But the inability to
state positively that Shakespeare knew the play
hardly lessens the significance of the strong parallel-
ism between it and the tragedy. Almost certainly it
was a source of *Timon of Athens.*

Besides relying upon these established sources it is
conceivable that Shakespeare enjoyed also an ac-
quaintance with certain secondary sources, and it is
possible that his interest in the Timon story was
increased by its currency in his own time. In Elizabethan literature Timon was regarded as a legitimate
and clearly defined type. Robert Greene alludes to
him, and Dekker and Nash slur at 'Timonists.' The
character crept into Lyly, and Shakespeare himself,
in *Love's Labour's Lost* (IV. iii. 170), has an apt

reference to the misanthrope: 'And critic Timon laugh
at idle toys.' It is possible, though by no means probable, that Shakespeare had read two plays of the
Renaissance, Boiardo's *Il Timone* (written about
1494) and Galeotto del Caretto's play of the same
name (written about 1497). Both these plays follow
Lucian closely, and add little to the Timon story
except an underplot. No hint of this underplot is
found in the tragedy. As Lucian's version of the tale
is reflected in Boiardo and Caretto, so Painter's story
has been followed by Sir Richard Barckley in his
Discourse on the Felicitie of Man (1598). Although
Shakespeare may well have been familiar with this
book, it is clear that he took nothing from it that he
might not have had from Painter's *Palace of Pleasure.*

APPENDIX B

HISTORY OF THE PLAY

Problematic in sources and authorship, *Timon of
Athens* has, in addition, a unique history as a printed
and acted play. No quartos exist; the play was first
printed in the Folio of 1623 in the section of the
Tragedies between *Romeo and Juliet* and *Julius
Cæsar.* On November 8, 1623, it was entered by the
publishers upon the Stationers' Register as one of the
plays 'not formerly entered to other men.'[1] The date
of composition of Shakespeare's part can be deter-
mined only by internal evidence. Various years have
been suggested between 1606 and 1610. The general

---

[1] No record exists of the acting of *Timon of Athens*
before 1623. Nevertheless, the stage directions seem to
indicate that the play had been acted. It is possible that
the tragedy was presented without success, and was soon
withdrawn.

likeness of the tragedy, in story and tone, to *King Lear* and *Coriolanus* fix it rather definitely in this period; while the theory that the idea of *Timon* occurred to Shakespeare while working on *Antony and Cleopatra* (see Appendix A) would place it about 1607-1608, a date upon which there has been some measure of agreement.

The dramatic history of *Timon of Athens* confirms the usual opinion of readers that it is not well suited for representation on the stage. It is, indeed, surprising that dramatic annals record no performance of the play, in its original form, even with only slight alterations, until towards the close of the eighteenth century. During the last quarter of the seventeenth century, however, there began to appear versions and alterations of the tragedy. Some of these included changes designed merely to please the taste of the time; others cut or expanded the original until it was almost unrecognizable; but all retain the central theme of Timon's misanthropy and much, also, of the indelible influence of Shakespeare. These versions, then, together with a few revivals of the play in its original form, constitute the stage-history of *Timon of Athens*.[1]

Probably the first performance of an alteration of *Timon of Athens* occurred in December, 1678, at Dorset Garden, when Thomas Shadwell's version of the play was acted under the title of *Timon of Athens, or The Man-Hater*. Thomas Betterton (1635?-1710) played the rôle of Timon. In the Dedication Shadwell says he has made the history of Timon 'into a play.' What changes he thought necessary to accomplish this result may be seen in the following excerpts from Genest: Shadwell 'introduces two ladies,—the one, with whom Timon was on the point of marriage, deserts him in his adversity—the other, whom he had

[1] The editor has in preparation a monograph supplying further details of the stage-history of the play and also some account of its history in Continental theatres.

himself deserted, sticks to him to the last—this love business is far from an improvement—Shadwell has likewise spoilt the character of Flavius, and made him desert his master. . . . Considerable additions are made to the part of Apemantus, but on the whole it is altered for the worse—in the 2d act, he is called a snarling stoick. . . . ' In the same act Shadwell also 'introduces some proper observations on bad poetry, applicable to his own times.' *The Jew of Venice* (1701) refers to the unpopularity of this production, but Genest declares it to have been the first of many performances of the play: 'It was afterwards revived, and continued on the acting list for many years—Downes indeed says it pleased the Court and City generally.'[1] At least five other productions of Shadwell's version took place between 1678 and 1745. On June 27, 1707, it was acted at the Haymarket Theatre with John Mills (d. 1736) as Timon and John Verbruggen (1688-1707) as Apemantus. Barton Booth (1681-1733) played Alcibiades, while the two female parts, unknown to Shakespeare, of Evandra and Melissa, were taken, respectively, by Mrs. Mary Porter (d. 1765) and Mrs. Bradshaw. Shadwell's version was also known in Ireland, for a record has survived of a performance at the Smock Alley Theater, Dublin, in the year 1715. The next[2] English per-

---

[1] The success of this version was due partially to the masque added by Henry Purcell.

[2] An amateur performance of *Timon of Athens* was given at the Clerkenwell charity school on February 6, 1711. John Honeycott, the master of the school, 'with the children of the school, publicly acted the play called "Timon of Athens," and by tickets signed by himself had invited several people to it.' For this venture Honeycott was rebuked by the Society for Promoting Christian Knowledge, the trustees of the school. (*Notes and Queries* 7th s. iii. See also Secretan's *Life of Robert Nelson*, London, 1860, 130.) Whether this was the original play of Shadwell's version is conjectural.

formance of this version occurred on December 8,
1720, at Drury Lane Theatre, Mills this time acting
the part of Apemantus and Booth that of Timon. It
was again seen at Covent Garden on May 1, 1733,[1]
with James Quin (1693-1766) as Apemantus. In
connection with the next performance at Drury Lane
on March 20, 1740, Genest says that the piece had not
been acted in three years, but no record is at hand to
prove the inference that the play was acted in 1737.
At this revival of 1740 Quin again played Apemantus;
Milward was Timon; Henry Woodward (1714-1777)
acted the rôle of the Poet; and Mrs. Hannah Pritch-
ard (1711-1768) had the part of Melissa. Shadwell's version was acted again, apparently for the last
time, on April 20, 1745, at the Covent Garden
Theatre.

A composite version, based upon both Shakespeare
and Shadwell, was published in 1768, by James
Dance, known to the stage as James Love. This play
was acted at about the same time at Richmond in a
theatre built by the author and his brother. No record exists, apparently, of a London performance, but
Biographia Dramatica says that the Richmond production was 'well received.'

An important eighteenth century alteration of
Timon of Athens was that written by Richard Cumberland, leader of the school of Sentimental Drama.
This saccharine version, in which Timon has a daughter Evanthe, beloved by Alcibiades, was acted at
Drury Lane on December 4, 1771. Horace Walpole,
who saw this production, thought that Cumberland had
'caught the manners and diction of the original so
exactly' that it was 'full as bad a play as it was before

---

[1] The influence of the play upon the stage at this time is
evidenced by the performance on December 5, 1733, of a
comedy of three acts, with songs, dealing with the theme of
Timon and his false friends, called *Timon in Love, or The
Innocent Theft*. This trifle was ascribed to C. J. Kelly.

he corrected it.' Radical changes from Shakespeare occur throughout the play, and the fifth act is almost entirely Cumberland's. In fact, Doran notes that this *Timon* has 'more of Cumberland and less of Shakespeare than the public could welcome.'

Shakespeare and Shadwell formed the basis for still another eighteenth century alteration by Thomas Hull (1728-1808), acted at Covent Garden Theatre on May 13, 1786. Joseph Holman (1764-1817) played Timon and Richard Wroughton (1748-1822) was 'a very good Apemantus.' Hull himself played the part of Flavius, and Mrs. Inchbald (1753-1821) that of Melissa. This production, too, was unsuccessful. It ought, says *The European Magazine* for May, 1786, 'to be consigned to oblivion.' 'The play,' says *Biographia Dramatica,* 'has been coldly received and has not been printed.'

The nineteenth century found less interest in new versions of *Timon of Athens* than in reviving the original play, often with elaborate scenic effects. But the play was always, as a whole, unsuccessful, and it becomes increasingly difficult not to acquiesce heartily in Sheridan's remark that 'it is calculated for the closet only, and cannot produce a great effect in representation.' Similarly Macready writes in his Diary: 'Looked at *Timon of Athens,* but it is (for the stage) only an incident with comments on it. The story is not complete enough—not furnished, I ought to say, with the requisite varieties of passion for a play; it is heavy and monotonous.' The first revival of the play in this century was Edmund Kean's at Drury Lane on October 28, 1816. George Lamb, in his Advertisement to this production, stated: 'The present attempt has been to restore Shakespeare on the stage, with no omissions than such as the refinement of manners rendered necessary.' Kean had the title rôle, and it was certainly due to his genius that the play was acted seven times. B. W. Proctor, in his *Life of Edmund*

Kean, praises the effectiveness of the play's latter dialogues when vitalized by Kean's passion, but says that even 'Kean was unable, by dint of his own single strength, to make it popular.' Writing in like vein, the editor of *The New Monthly Magazine* for December, 1816, declares that 'till the conclusion of the third act he [Kean] had very little opportunity of distinguishing himself.' The same magazine also says that 'the tragedy [is] got up in splendid style; the banquet scene in particular is superb.'

Thirty-five years later, on September 15, 1851, at Sadler's Wells, Samuel Phelps 'produced with great splendor Shakespeare's Timon of Athens, and again made a tremendous effect on play-goers generally in the character of Timon. Old habitués and the critics who remembered Edmund Kean in this character all said Phelps surpassed him.' This production was acted about forty times between its first night and the following Christmas.

On October 11, 1856, Phelps revived the production with new scenery 'not only archæologically correct, but picturesquely beautiful.' Alcibiades' attack upon Athens was 'a masterpiece of effect and contrivance.' This and the earlier rendering of the play concluded 'with a beautiful seaside view, where the tomb of Timon is the conspicuous object, before which the army of the invader is drawn up in reverence.' Frank Marshall, in the *Henry Irving Shakespeare,* says: 'Francis Guest Tomlins, secretary of the original Shakespeare Society, instituted comparisons between the Shakespearean revivals at Sadler's Wells and those by Charles Kean at the Princess's, wholly to the credit of the former. At the head of the Princess's was a showman who as lavishly illustrates Pizarro as Macbeth; at that of Sadler's Wells was an artist who assigned fervour and genius predominance over archæology.' This production of *Timon* pleased Professor Morley, who has recorded his impressions in

his *Journal of a London Playgoer:* 'Timon of Athens,'
he says, 'is always a poem to the Sadler's Wells audi-
ence.' Of Phelps' performance in the rôle of Timon
he adds: 'His . . . acting treats the character as an
ideal, as the central figure in a mystery. As the liberal Athenian lord, his gestures are large, his move-
ments free—out of himself everything pours, towards
himself he will draw nothing.'

When *Timon of Athens* was next acted is uncertain. *The Atheneum* of May 28, 1904, says that
Charles Calvert, the actor-manager, staged the tragedy about twenty years after Phelps' production, at
Manchester. Professor Ward, however, in his list of
Calvert's Shakespearean revivals, begun at the Theatre Royal, Manchester, in 1864, does not include
Timon of Athens. It is quite possible, then, that the
next performance of the play was that at Stratford-
on-Avon, in the annual series of Shakespearean plays
undertaken by F. R. Benson, beginning Monday,
April 18, 1892. *Timon of Athens* was acted three
times during the week, once on Friday, and twice on
Saturday, the poet's birthday. A three-act version
was given. *Timon* was again produced, apparently in
similar form, in London, at the Court Theatre, on
May 18, 1904, when it enjoyed a run of some ten
nights. *The London Times* of May 19 praises the
production, but notes that there is 'no "female interest" in the play, and [that] even the ladies Timandra
and Phrynia "mistresses to Alcibiades" have been on
this occasion virtually reduced to dumb-show.' In
conclusion the reviewer adds: 'There is a lovely ballet,
and a Cupid who might have strayed out of Offen-
bach's *Belle Hélène.*' Altogether the *Times* finds this
Timon 'an olio of attractions.' On the other hand,
The Atheneum declares that the performance pos-
sessed 'little interest beyond that of curiosity.'

Perhaps the earliest performance of *Timon of*

Athens in America occurred when an adaptation by
N. H. Bannister was acted for the first time at the
Franklin Theatre in New York City on April 8, 1839.
We are told that Richard Mansfield considered the
production of the tragedy, but no proof is available
that the play has been recently acted on the American
stage except in a series of performances by Mr. Fred-
erick Warde when on tour in 1910.

APPENDIX C

AUTHORSHIP OF THE PLAY

The exact circumstances of the writing of *Timon of
Athens* will probably remain conjectural, but that the
play is not wholly Shakespeare's creation is certain.
Double authorship is constantly proclaimed by singu-
larities of workmanship and by technical problems
involving inconsistencies in character and action.
Regular and highly irregular verse, rhymed and un-
rhymed lines, dignified prose and prose that is
absurdly flat follow each other in capricious fashion.
Poetry as lofty as that of *King Lear* is linked to dog-
gerel, and scenes unquestionably written by Shakespeare suddenly become inane under the influence of
another hand. By means of internal evidence of this
character scholars have tried to determine how much
of the play was written by Shakespeare and how much
by the unknown assistant.

The ascriptions differ in detail, but there is some
agreement regarding the portions of the tragedy
attributable to Shakespeare. About the first one hundred and seventy-five lines of the play are admittedly
his (I. i. 1-177). In the passage between the entrance
of Apemantus and that of Alcibiades (I. i. 178-249)
only the first ten lines have generally been assigned

to Shakespeare.[1] The rest of the scene (250-296)
was probably written by Shakespeare, with the exception of about eighteen lines of dialogue between the
two lords and Apemantus (266-283).[2] Bad verse and
blunders have marked the second scene as non-Shakespearean.[3] The first scene of the second act is Shakespeare's (II. i.). The second scene of this act is, by
substantial agreement, conceded to be Shakespeare's
as far as the entrance of Apemantus and the Fool (II.
ii. 1-45),[4] and there is approximately similar agreement that the episode introduced by this entrance is
spurious (46-132).[5] The remainder of the scene,
approximately (133-243), is usually attributed to
Shakespeare except ten prose lines that intrude upon
the verse (196-205).[6] The first three scenes of the

[1] Fleay was supported in this belief by Hudson, Rolfe,
Gollancz, and White. Wright thinks it likely that Shakespeare was the author of the entire passage.

[2] Concerning this passage Fleay argued that the unknown
author retained the two lords on the stage to jeer at
Apemantus, preparing more naturally for the cynic's entrance in the next scene, when he appears 'dropping after
all, discontentedly, like himself.' (I. ii. S. d.) Wright con-
siders the passage Shakespeare's.

[3] Among other crudities and errors, Wright mentions
the following: Ventidius desires to pay his debt to Timon,
thus nullifying the dramatic effect of Timon's later request
for Ventidius' aid; and in the last act, senators are announced but do not enter.

[4] Fleay, Hudson, Rolfe, Gollancz, White, and Wright
agree on this point of division.

[5] In this passage occurs a typical problem: The Steward
urges the duns to await Timon's answer, and with the words,
'Pray, draw near,' is escorting them off, when Apemantus
approaches. Whereupon, one of the duns says, 'Stay, stay!'
The Steward leaves, but the duns remain throughout the
next episode. Johnson suggests that at this point an entire
scene is missing.

[6] Wright advances the theory that all of these lines, save
one, are Shakespeare's. Gollancz believes lines 45-124 (approximately) to be non-Shakespearean.

third act are probably interpolations (III. i., ii., iii.).[1]
The commonplace fourth scene is not genuine (III.
iv.) ;[2] nor is the ill-motivated scene showing Alcibiades
before the Senate (III. v.). In the sixth scene (III.
vi.) I think we can safely assign only Timon's de-
nunciation (99-116) to Shakespeare, though more
considerable portions have sometimes been ascribed to
him.[3] 'From the fourth act on,' as Wright says, 'the
play may be called Shakspere's.' The first scene of
this act is almost certainly his (IV. i.) and about the
first thirty lines of the second scene (IV. ii. 1-29) may
possibly have been touched by his hand.[4] The important third scene (IV. iii.) has evoked marked differ-
ences of opinion. Although it is generally conceded
that almost the first three hundred lines are Shakespeare's (IV. iii. 1-292), the exact ending of the interpolated passage that follows (292 ff.) is disputed.
Fleay would end it at about line 362, and others have
adopted his conclusion; Wright, however, believes that
Shakespeare's hand is not again discernible until
about line 376. The rest of this episode, as far as the
entrance of the Banditti, is conceded to be Shakespeare's (376-400). It has been customary to regard
a few lines at the opening and a few lines at the clos-
ing of the Banditti episode as spurious, but it is quite
possible that the whole passage is genuine (401-

1 Wright develops an ingenious theory that the first two
of these scenes are Shakespeare's. White holds that Shakespeare wrote some dozen lines in the first scene (III. i. 54-
66).

2 Three characters, Titus, Hortensius, and Philotus, appear here for the only time in the play. The introduction of
a character called Lucius, apparently not the Lucius of the
next act, is also puzzling.

3 Hudson assigns to Shakespeare all lines spoken while
Timon is on the stage (28-116).

4 Hudson and Wright include these lines in their ascriptions, but Fleay and Rolfe do not.

466).[1] The rest of the scene is probably interpolated (467-545).[2] The first scene of the fifth act with the possible exception of the introduction (1-59) was written by Shakespeare.[3] The second and fourth scenes are likewise his; only the third scene bears no trace of his workmanship.[4]

Concerning the double authorship of *Timon of Athens* there have arisen three distinct theories:

(1) *Timon of Athens* of the Folio represents Shakespeare's work as interpolated and corrupted by the players. In his lectures of 1815, Coleridge stated his belief that the play was Shakespeare's throughout, and that when first written it was one of the Poet's most complete performances.[5] He explained the un-

[1] Hudson maintains that Shakespeare wrote approximately the first four hundred and sixty-four lines of this scene.

[2] Wright ascribes to Shakespeare approximately lines 479-508 and 530-543.

[3] Wright thinks it possible that Shakespeare wrote these lines, since they constitute the introduction to his own scene.

[4] A characteristic problem occurs in this act in connection with the entrance of the Poet and Painter. At IV. iii. 356, Apemantus says: 'Yonder comes a poet and a painter.' Yet these characters do not actually enter until about two hundred lines later at the beginning of the fifth act. Thus the leisurely approach of the Poet and Painter becomes an absurdity. To meet the difficulty Hudson substituted 'parcel of soldiers' for 'poet and painter.' Wright explains the confusion by declaring that Apemantus' words occur in a spurious passage; in this case the premature announcement was made by the interpolator.

[5] This was the conviction of many German scholars, among them Schlegel, Gervinus, and Ulrici. Elze, however, believed that parts of the play were due to an old *Timon* (*William Shakespeare*, 1876); Wendlandt thought that *Shakespeare* had left part of the play in rough draft (*Jahrbuch*, 1888); Kullmann suggested that there had been three authors (*Archiv für Litteraturgeschichte*, 1882); and Bulthaupt ascribed only a small part of the play to Shakespeare. 'I conjecture,' says Ulrici, ' . . . that Shakespeare originally made a rapid and hurried sketch of "Timon of

usual versification on the ground that the play had
been injured by the actors, and was of the opinion
that the editors of 1623 saw only a mutilated copy of
the original.[1] This theory would be more tenable if
there existed positive proof that the play was fre-
quently acted before 1623. But such proof is not to
be had. Opportunity for interpolation by the players
was almost certainly limited. This theory has, generally speaking, given way before more vigorous
hypotheses.

(2) Shakespeare rewrote or revised an earlier
Timon of Athens, the work of an inferior dramatist.
This theory, having its genesis in a belief of Farmer's
that there had been an earlier popular play with
Timon as a hero, was first advanced by Knight in
1838: '*Timon* was a play originally produced by an
artist very inferior to Shakespeare, [and] probably
retained possession of the stage for some time in its
first form; . . . It has come down to us not wholly
rewritten but so far remodelled that entire scenes of
Shakespeare have been substituted for entire scenes of
the elder play.'[2] Delius gave this theory its fullest
development in 1867.[3] With slight divergences of
opinion Delius' view has been supported by the Cam-
bridge Editors, Staunton, Dyce, Nicholson, Evans,
and others. 'The original play,' say the first of these,
'on which Shakespeare worked, must have been written, for the most part, either in prose or in very irreg-

Athens," only that this was done with greater hurry and
carelessness than usual . . . but that subsequently—after
the piece had been brought upon the stage—he found himself nevertheless obliged to work out some parts with more
care.' (*Shakespeare's Dramatic Art,* Vol. I, p. 523.)

[1] A passage in the third act (III. iii. 32-34) may be inter-
preted as a satire upon the Puritans. Coleridge considered
this an actor's interpolation.

[2] *Pictorial Edition,* 1838.

[3] *Jahrbuch der deutschen Shakespeare Gesellschaft,*
1867, pp. 335 ff.

ular verse.' Evans' comment may be taken as typical
of the theory: 'We assume that during his reading of
Plutarch Shakespeare's attention was arrested by the
story of Timon; that it struck him that the character
of Timon might be made effective for the stage, and
not having time or inclination to work up a complete
plot into a regular five-act play he availed himself of
a "Timon" which was in the hands of the theatre at
the time. . . . Accordingly he rewrote about half of
it, and hastily revised the rest, leaving this for the
most part untouched, but inserting or altering a few
lines or phrases here and there. But before he had
had time to give the whole a final revision it was
called for by the manager, and hurried upon the
boards. These assumptions will account both for the
general unity of the plan as well as for the signs of
incomplete revision observable here and there.'[1] In
quality of argument, and in the support afforded it by
eminent scholars, this theory will probably remain
important. It has, however, been overshadowed by
the third hypothesis.

(3) Shakespeare wrote the main portions of *Timon
of Athens*—which was completed or revised by an
inferior dramatist. Verplanck, the American scholar,
led the way for this theory in 1847, when he wrote:
'It is like . . . a work left incomplete and finished by
another hand, inferior, though not without skill, and
working on the conceptions of the greater master.'
In the same connection he adds: 'The hypothesis
which I should offer . . . is this: Shakespeare
adopted the canvas of *Timon's* story as a fit vehicle
for poetic satire . . . while, as to the rest, he con-
tented himself with a rapid and careless composition
of some scenes and probably on others (such as that of
Alcibiades with the Senate) contenting himself with

[1] *The Works of William Shakespeare,* edited by Henry
Irving and Frank A. Marshall, Introduction to *Timon of
Athens.*

simply sketching out the substance of an intended dialogue to be afterwards elaborated.'[1] In 1869 this
conception of the authorship was further discussed by
Tschischwitz.[2] The theory culminated in 1874 in the
analysis and argument of Fleay who stated strongly
his confidence in Shakespeare's priority.[3] He con-
cludes his Essay as follows: 'The *essential* part of this
paper is the proof that the Shakspere part of this
play was written *before* the other part.' Among the
critics who have, in the main, subscribed to this theory
are Rolfe, Hudson, Deighton, Gollancz, and Furni-
vall. Hudson declares that 'whatsoever may be
judged of this theory in other respects it seems to
make clear work with the question why there should
be in this case so great discrepancy of style and execu-
tion joined with such general unity of purpose and
movement.'[4] Apropos of the second theory, that
Shakespeare revised an earlier play, the same critic
says: 'Shakespeare's approved severity of taste and
strength of judgment at that period of his life,
together with his fulness and availability of resource,
would hardly have endured to retain certain parts in
so crude and feeble a state as we here find them.'[5]
This belief in Shakespeare's priority has grown, and,
unless some new subversive evidence appears, can
hardly be shaken.[6]

1 *The Illustrated Shakespeare,* edited by G. C. Verplanck
(New York, 1847), Introduction to *Timon of Athens.*

2 *Jahrbuch,* 1869, 160-197.

3 *Transactions of the New Shakspere Society,* 1874.

4 *Shakespeare's Complete Works,* edited by H. N. Hudson, Introduction to *Timon of Athens.*

5 *Ibid.*

6 E. H. Wright, in *The Authorship of Timon of Athens,*
elaborates upon the theory of Shakespeare's priority. Rea-
soning that nine lines of a ten-line prose passage (II. ii.
194-204) are genuine, Wright is enabled to advance the
theory that the germane scenes are also Shakespeare's (III.
i., and III. ii.). If these two scenes are spurious, as they

Although the dual authorship of *Timon of Athens*
has been long admitted, comparatively little has been
done to identify the second author. The inferior
parts of the play have been variously ascribed—with
meagre evidence, in every case—to Thomas Heywood
(d. 1650?), George Wilkins (fl. 1607), John Day
(fl. 1606), and Cyril Tourneur (1575?-1626). Verplanck surmises that when the play was wanted by
Heming and Condell 'some literary artist like Heywood was invited to fill up the accessory and subordi-
nate parts of the play upon the author's own outline,
and this was done, or attempted to be done, in the
manner of the great original, as far as possible, but
with distinction of his varieties of style.'[1] Delius
believed that both *Pericles* and *Timon* showed the

have been usually considered, Shakespeare's share of the
play has been inadequately motivated. If, on the other
hand, these two scenes are from his pen, Shakespeare himself has motivated Timon's misanthropy, and his priority
in composition is rendered more likely. (A second apparent
gap in the play has been the lack of motivation for the
assistance given Timon by Alcibiades. Wright shows how
the interpolator tried to close this gap, and suggests how
Shakespeare himself may have planned to fill it.) As an
additional argument for Shakespeare's priority Wright also
notes that every point at which the play follows a source
'falls within a scene that Shakespeare wrote—that every
episode or line for which a source is known comes from his
pen.' In concluding his argument for Shakespeare's priority Wright says: 'Ten spurious scenes and passages scat-
tered through Shakspere's play and filling one third of it;
and Shakspere never using them, never counting on them,
never, except to suggest one (III. vi. 60: "Alcibiades is
banished.") making a mention of them,—unaware of them.
Lift them bodily from the play, and not a word will tell
that they were ever in it. The fact is final. Those scenes
and passages were no nucleus around which Shakspere built
his play. They were extensions to the play he had already
built.'

[1] *The Illustrated Shakespeare,* edited by G. C. Verplanck,
(New York, 1847), Introduction to *Timon of Athens.*

hand of George Wilkins, but his evidence is uncon-
vincing.[1] Wright, in commenting upon this latter
theory, declares, with reason, that 'the nearer a
reviewer comes to thinking that George Wilkins wrote
the regular though wooden verse of the first two acts
of *Pericles,* the farther he will be from a belief that
the same man wrote the highly irregular verse of the
interpolations in *Timon.*'[2]

Fleay does not press his theory strongly, but
points out that in ratio of rhyme to blank verse, irregularities of length, and double endings, *Timon of
Athens* resembles closely *The Revenger's Tragedy*
(1607) by Tourneur. He notes that Tourneur is fond
of quoting Latin.

Fleay subjoins passages from *The Revenger's
Tragedy* which he finds to be in exactly the strain of
the unknown author of *Timon of Athens,*[3] and states
positively his belief that 'Cyril Tourneur was the only
person connected with the King's Company who could
have written the other part of the play.'[4] It should
be observed that Fleay's identification of Tourneur as
reviser of *Timon* loses force if Tourneur's authorship
of *The Revenger's Tragedy* be denied.

1 *Jahrbuch,* 1867, p. 175.
2 *The Authorship of Timon of Athens,* p. 101.
3 Dodsley's Edition, pp. 322, 384.
4 See *Transactions of the New Shakspere Society,* 1874,
pp. 138-139.

APPENDIX D

The Text of the Present Edition

Only the Folio text of *Timon of Athens* has survived. The text of the present volume is, by permission of the Oxford University Press, that of the Oxford Shakespeare, edited by the late W. J. Craig, except for the following deviations:

1. In almost every case the stage directions of the Folio have been restored. A few obvious errors in these have been corrected. Necessary or helpful modern stage directions have been added within square brackets.

2. Craig's punctuation has been normalized, as well as the spelling of a very few words: e.g., villainy (villany), court'sies (curtsies), basin (bason), again (agen).

3. Various changes in wording have been made, usually with the purpose of following more closely the Folio text. In the following list of verbal variations from Craig's text, the new readings precede the colon, while Craig's versions are given after it. When concerned in the change, the Folio authority has been indicated.

[Dramatis Personæ] F (Spelling modernized and modern additions bracketed): Dramatis Personæ (entirely modern).

I. i. 42	moe F: more	So also: II. i. 7; II. ii. 117; IV. iii. 400, 439
	163	ye F: you So also: III. iv. 46
	269	most F: more
	283	o' the ass F: of an ass
ii. 32	for 't F: for it	
	41	sees 'em not F: sees them not
	112	ere 't F: ere it
	134	Taste, touch, and smell: Taste, touch, smell

136 They're F: They are
151 't has F: it has
169 tell him—well, i' faith, I should—: tell him
      well, i' faith, I should,
213 Than such that do F: Than such as do
II. ii. 202 'em F: them
231 ingeniously F: ingenuously
III. i. 32 from 't F: from it
 ii. 58 done 't F: done it
 iii. 21 and 'mongst lords I be thought a fool: and
      I 'mongst lords be thought a fool. ['I'
      not in Folio.]
22 I'd F: I had
23 He'd: He had
 iv. 46 ye F: you
 v. 50 fellow F: felon
108 I'm F: I am
 vi. 22 of you F: you (misprint)
IV. ii. 33 to live F: so live
42 blest F: bless'd See also: IV. iii. 544
 iii. 32 heads F: head
216 bade F: bid
330 t' attain F: to attain
454 not F: no
479 Has F: He hath
486 me, I; all: me; ay all
V. i. 4 he's F: he is
18 travail F: travel
75 travail'd F: travell'd
115 would'st F: would
117 you F: ye
153 it F: its
158 blot F: block
 iii. 4 read F: rear'd
     there F: here

APPENDIX E

Suggestions for Collateral Reading

Charles Knight: *Preface to Timon of Athens* in the *Pictorial Edition,* 1838.

Timon, A Play, edited by A. Dyce, 1842. (The Timon comedy, printed from the original manuscript.)

G. C. Verplanck: *Preface to Timon of Athens* in *Shakespeare's Plays,* 1847.

Nikolaus Delius: *Über Shakespeare's Timon of Athens,* in the *Jahrbuch der deutschen Shakespeare Gesellschaft,* vol. ii., 1867. *Über Shakespeare's Pericles* in the *Jahrbuch,* vol. iii., 1868.

F. G. Fleay: In *Transactions of the New Shakspere Society,* 130-194, 1874: *On the Authorship of Timon of Athens,* followed by *The Life of Tymon of Athens, As Written by W. Shakspere. Shakespeare Manual,* 49, 1876. *Life and Work of Shakspere,* 242-244, 1886.

A. W. Ward: *A History of English Dramatic Literature,* vol. ii., 177-180, 1899.

W. H. Clemons: *The Sources of Timon of Athens,* in the Princeton University Bulletin, 208-223, September, 1904. (A complete descriptive record of the sources of the play.)

J. Q. Adams: *Timon of Athens and the Irregularities in the First Folio,* in the *Journal of English and Germanic Philology,* 53-63, January, 1908. (An excellent summary of the most important textual problems of the play, with particular reference to its authorship.)

Ernest Hunter Wright: *The Authorship of Timon of Athens,* in *Columbia University Studies in English,*

New York, 1910. (The most comprehensive study of *Timon of Athens* available.)

Other helpful editions of *Timon of Athens* are W. J. Rolfe's (1882); Frank A. Marshall's in vol. vii. of the *Henry Irving Shakespeare* (1888) (containing the most complete stage-history of the play); K. Deighton's *Timon of Athens* in *The Works of Shakespeare* (very fully annotated); and the edition in the *Aldus Shakespeare,* with comments of H. N. Hudson, I. Gollancz, C. H. Herford, and others.

Students interested in later versions of *Timon of Athens* on the stage will find suggestive comment in the following: John Genest's *Some Account of the English Stage, from the Restoration in 1660 to 1830,* 1832 (versions of the play by Shadwell, Cumberland, Hull, and Love are discussed under the dates of performance); S. T. Williams' *Richard Cumberland,* 88-91, 1917 (Cumberland's version); B. W. Proctor's *Life of Edmund Kean,* 178-179, 1835; W. M. Phelps' and John Forbes-Robertson's *Life and Life-Work of Samuel Phelps,* 262 ff., 1886.

INDEX OF WORDS GLOSSED

(Figures in full-faced type refer to page-numbers)

close: 89 (V. i. 210)
cog: 85 (V. i. 100)
coil: 22 (I. ii. 239)
cold-moving: 34 (II. ii. 222)
comes off: 2 (I. i. 30)
comfortable: 79 (IV. iii. 500)
common lag: 55 (III. vi. 91)
complete: 35 (III. i. 10)
composture: 77 (IV. iii. 447)
compt: 25 (II. i. 35)
conceit: 92 (V. iv. 14)
conceive . . . fairest: 39 (III. ii. 60)
conceptious: 68 (IV. iii. 188)
conditions: 66 (IV. iii. 140)
confectionary: 70 (IV. iii. 261)
confound: 73 (IV. iii. 340)
confounding: 57 (IV. i. 20)
confusion: 65 (IV. iii. 128)
confusion: 73 (IV. iii. 326)
consideration: 68 (IV. iii. 197)
continuate: 1 (I. i. 11)
convert: 57 (IV. i. 7)
copies: 42 (III. iii. 32)
Corinth: 28 (II. ii. 72)
corporate: 33 (II. ii. 214)
corse: 95 (V. iv. 70)
counterfeit: 84 (IV. iii. 113)
counterfeit: 84 (V. i. 85)
courage: 42 (III. iii. 24)
crisp: 67 (IV. iii. 184)
crown'd: 32 (II. ii. 191)
cunning: 68 (IV. iii. 210)
curiosity: 72 (IV. iii. 303)

dangerous notes: 15 (I. ii. 53)
date-broke: 27 (II. ii. 38)
dear: 75 (IV. iii. 384; V. i. 233)
dearest: 6 (I. i. 125)
deed of saying: 82 (V. i. 29)
depart: 11 (I. i. 264)

depraved: 18 (I. ii. 147)
depraves: 18 (I. ii. 147)
dich: 16 (I. ii. 74)
discharged: 26 (II. ii. 12)
discovery: 82 (V. i. 39)
disfurnish: 39 (III. ii. 49)
dividant: 60 (IV. iii. 5)
doit: 10 (I. i. 218)
domestic awe: 57 (IV. i. 17)
dost . . . not: 65 (IV. iii. 132)
doubt: 19 (I. ii. 161)
doubtfully: 65 (IV. iii. 122)
draught: 85 (V. i. 107)
drift: 3 (I. i. 46)
dropping after all: 13 (I. ii. S. d.)

earnest: 62 (IV. iii. 47)
embossed: 90 (V. i. 222)
englutted: 32 (II. ii. 176)
entertain: 79 (IV. iii. 498)
entertain'd: 21 (I. ii. 194)
example: 77 (IV. iii. 441)
exceptless: 79 (IV. iii. 504)

fact: 48 (III. v. 16)
factions: 50 (III. v. 74)
fail: 87 (V. i. 153)
faint: 42 (III. iii. 25)
fairly: 20 (I. ii. 185)
falling-from: 76 (IV. iii. 404)
familiars . . . fortunes: 58 (IV. ii. 10)
fang: 61 (IV. iii. 23)
fees: 55 (III. vi. 90)
fell: 62 (IV. iii. 61)
fellows: 59 (IV. ii. 18)
files: 90 (V. ii. 1)
filths: 57 (IV. i. 6)
fit: 83 (V. i. 59)
fitly: 47 (III. iv. 113)
fix'd: 1 (I. i. 9)
flamen: 66 (IV iii. 156)
flush: 92 (V. iv. 8)
fond: 15 (I. ii. 66)